Legal Disclaimer

The information contained within this book is strictly for educational purposes. If you wish to apply ideas contained in this book, you are taking full responsibility for your actions. The author has made every effort to ensure that the accuracy of the information within this book was correct at time of publication. The author does not assume and hereby disclaims any liability to any party for any loss, damage, or disruption caused by errors or omissions, whether such errors or omissions result from accident, negligence, or any other cause. This book does not provide legal advice and does not create an attorney-client relationship. If you need legal advice, please contact an attorney directly.

Online and Under Attack

Online and Under Attack

WHAT EVERY BUSINESS NEEDS TO DO NOW TO
MANAGE CYBER RISK AND WIN ITS CYBER WAR

John Farley

ISBN: 1542342902
ISBN-13: 9781542342902

Contents

Prologue

G rowing up in Bayside, Queens, in the shadow of the mighty Manhattan skyline, I often found myself rooting for the underdog. It was only fitting. I lived in New York City but technically *outside* the city. The millionaires lived there, while we took buses and trains to get our piece of the action. Perhaps a victim of geography, it was only natural that I gravitated to becoming a fan of the New York Mets, who played only a few miles from my home. The time was the 1970s and early 1980s. At the time, the crosstown rival Yankees were winning World Series games, while my lowly Mets were perennial losers. The Mets were a big-market team in a big city with a big budget, but they always found a way to lose. When they were not losing, they were busy making terrible decisions by making terrible trades. Shrugging off the stats, I constantly found myself on the Q27 bus on the way to Shea Stadium, the dusty old relic left over from the 1964 World's Fair. The Mets were a talented, hard-partying, unapologetic, borderline criminal team, full of characters larger than life, who reminded me of my own friends from Bayside. On a cold October night in Queens, they roared past the Boston Red Sox for their first championship in seventeen years. My loyalty to that motley crew paid off in 1986.

My professional career has moved in much the same way. I am a cyber-risk management consultant for corporations. One might argue, however, that working for some large, multinational conglomerate is not working for an underdog. Instead, some might argue that I am working for companies with deep pockets with which they can easily manage cyber risk. I would beg to differ. In the past three years, many major corporations with millions of dollars devoted to cybersecurity have fallen victim to cybercrime in dramatic fashion. Just like my New York Mets, these companies have proven that big budgets can't always buy success. In 2013 cyber thieves stole forty million credit cards from Target. In 2015 Anthem was compromised to the tune of eighty million people's personally identifiable information. In 2016 it was revealed that hackers took the login credentials of a staggering one billion customers of Yahoo. The list goes on and on. Nobody has come up with a magic bullet, and the fight to secure data seems to be an uphill battle, if not an impossible task. Many businesses, especially the larger ones, are charged with the unenviable task of successfully fending off attempts to penetrate networks hundreds if not thousands of times per day. Nobody hears about the unsung heroes who toil in the back rooms of their IT security departments. They have to win *all day*, *every day*. The hackers, by contrast, need to succeed only *once*. When they do, the hammer comes down, and the organization pays up. It's hardly a fair game.

These massive, resource-rich companies are actually *losing* to mysterious underground hackers, some of whom may not have more than a few thousand dollars to their name. Ironically, Anthem, Target, Yahoo, and countless other big businesses are today's underdogs, and they need all the help they can get.

CHAPTER 1

Introduction

Every once in a while, a generation of people rises to the challenges of their day in spectacular fashion. Tom Brokaw wrote of one such group of people in his popular book *The Greatest Generation*. Mr. Brokaw eloquently writes of an entire American generation that suffered through the economic calamity that was the Great Depression. As unemployment reached 25 percent in the 1930s, families struggled to put food on the table and lost businesses and homes. Then in 1941, these same people were suddenly thrust into a world war. During World War II, farm boys who had never left their small towns found themselves armed with machine guns in the hills of Italy, parachuting out of planes over France, and swimming for their lives as they jumped off burning navy vessels in the South Pacific, literally fighting off sharks as they swam. Fathers were ripped away from their families, and many never came home. Mothers entered the workforce for the first time to fill important roles left vacant by the men who went to war. These women literally changed the workplace forever, almost overnight. Through courage to directly engage the enemy, determination, and a willingness to embrace change during times of uncertainty, America emerged from the dark days of the 1930s and 1940s stronger than ever before. The average citizens who helped drive us to victory were, in a word, heroic.

One challenge that the Greatest Generation did not have to contend with was the struggles brought on by the information age we all grapple with today. My late mother, Maureen Farley, never owned a laptop or a smartphone. A tough Irish Catholic born into a large family in 1932, she saw no need for these expensive and cumbersome devices and never took the time to fully understand them. As a child growing up in the Bronx, New York, she knew that when the streetlights came on, it was time to go home. Those streetlights still work just fine today, she reasoned. Why then, she wondered, do parents need to buy cell phones for themselves and all their kids and text them when it nears their curfew? Landline telephones existed then as they do today and could be used in an emergency. She kept up with current events in large part by reading several newspapers a day. If she needed a radio or TV, they were available, too, but were never really a necessity. Forget trying to explain social media. To her, Facebook and LinkedIn were words from a foreign language she was never going to learn to translate.

Maureen Farley, in one sense, was a very fortunate woman. She was largely immune to the cyber threats that come with engaging and processing information through the Internet and technology. She didn't have to play the game. Most of us, by contrast, have been *thrown into* the game and will play it for the foreseeable future, like it or not. On a daily basis, at work and at play, we fire up laptops and charge smartphones in a daily ritual. Texts fly, e-mails fill in-boxes, and social media takes over lives as the dominant form of communication today. As we leave our offices and homes, the beat goes on. We know we shouldn't text and drive, but as we pull to a stop at the red light, we say the "red light prayer," heads bowed to the smartphone god that rests on our laps.

With all the conveniences that modern technology brings, in recent years we have come to terms with the fact that all is not great in the online world. Over the past twenty or so years, threats have emerged and evolved in ways we never could have imagined. Businesses have been hit particularly hard, and the evolution of the threat to commerce has proven to be very real.

In the 1990s, the biggest worry for an IT department was a virus or a network issue that, at its worst, meant a minor interruption in business. It was a speed bump that was quickly remedied in the back rooms of the IT department. These issues rarely ever rose to the middle-management level, much less the C-suite. As we approached the year

2000, the concept of Y2K emerged and rang alarms bells we were not used to hearing. Some felt that when the clock struck midnight on January 1, 2000, much of our technology would succumb to an inherent flaw in its systems, leading to mass chaos. Thankfully, that never happened, and the year 2000 was celebrated on New Year's Day without a hitch. What did happen, unfortunately, led some to believe that there were no real threats associated with technology, and anyone who raised cyber threat concerns was just crying wolf. Y2K became a running joke.

As we entered the mid-2000s, that mind-set started to change. Criminal activity emerged in the form of credit-card fraud and ID theft. The earliest form of hackers successfully exploited large databases of sensitive data. A number of large retailers fell victim to hackers, leading to millions of dollars in credit-card fraud. Around that same time, regulatory authorities began to introduce regulation aimed at businesses that held sensitive data in their networks. Those companies that failed to comply with network-security standards were pursued by regulators with litigation and ultimately hit with fines. Since that time, we have seen continued regulation, and more authority figures are getting into the act of enforcement. Plaintiff attorneys have also joined the melee by pursuing companies via class-action lawsuits on behalf of those whose personal information may have been compromised. Meanwhile, the methods of the data thieves continue to evolve, and the cat-and-mouse game they play with those employed in cybersecurity continues to play out. If you ask who is winning the game, you might get a different answer depending on whom you ask. Concern is growing, as news stories about network-security incidents and private information being exposed seem to come at us on a daily basis. There are many who repeat an often-heard saying: There are three types of companies: those that have been hacked, those that don't know they have been hacked, and those that have been hacked again.

Now we are faced with the concept of the "Internet of Things," the idea that many of the products we use on a daily basis will be connected to the Internet. A 2015 report by the Federal Trade Commission (FTC) indicates that as of 2015 there were twenty-five billion Internet-connected devices. By 2020, the FTC is projecting that number to double to fifty billion. It's not just laptops and smartphones. Security systems, temperature controls, automobiles, and medical devices are all Internet reliant. More concerning, most of our critical infrastructure is Internet connected. Nuclear power plants, satellites, vast industrial control systems, electric power grids, and the financial markets all depend on a secure Internet to function properly. If they are all connected to the Internet, then aren't they also as vulnerable? The answer, unfortunately, is yes.

Unlike the enemies of the Greatest Generation, today's cyber enemy waves no flag and wears no uniform. As the Pearl Harbor attack unfolded, we knew within minutes it was the Japanese, as their country's symbol was boldly emblazoned on the sides of the planes as they flew low over the harbor. Our modern-day cyberattacks stand in stark contrast. Many times, we are not sure exactly who carried out the cyberattack that penetrated our networks. Was it a nation-state? An organized crime ring? A kid working from his parents' basement? The required response is equally unclear. Will the government help the private sector? Which authority? Do we invade a country that we believe was behind the attack, even though it adamantly denies any involvement? How do we prove that a nation or a person was behind the keyboard? Should we take matters into our own hands and hack them back? Unfortunately, attribution for cybercrimes is difficult, and there are probably more questions than there are answers.

This book is not meant to scare anyone or perpetuate myths for the sake of sensationalizing an often-misunderstood threat. It is instead an attempt to lay out where we stand today in terms of everyday digital threats to corporations and the realistic ways they might be able to fight back. For many, it is unchartered territory, and the world seems to be crying out for a cyber-risk management playbook to guide them. So strap on your cyber-risk seatbelt and join me on what will be a wild ride to try and tame the wild beast that is cyber risk.

CHAPTER 2

Know Your Enemy: A View from the Hacker's Perspective

There is an old saying that remains very relevant in today's world of cyber-risk management: *Keep your friends close, but keep your enemies closer.* Getting to know the cybercriminals is the first essential step in figuring out how to defend against them. Understanding who they are targeting, what they are after, and how they are carrying out their crimes will help any organization prepare for an attack. Financial gains, political agendas, and sheer emotions are some of the common motivators. Physical location of the attackers may also give clues to their agenda, since some of the more sophisticated organized-crime rings tend to operate in a handful of countries. The hacker's host country may also make matters difficult to investigate and criminals difficult to prosecute. What kind of expertise do they have? Who is funding them? Which law-enforcement agency would be best to contact for help? Will the hacker's host-country government authorities help or hinder the efforts of the victims and the law-enforcement authorities who are trying to bring them to justice?

We have categorized cyberattackers into four distinct groups:

Criminal Hackers

The most common, and probably most feared, cyber-criminals are those who are in the game solely for financial gain. They have been around for decades and have successfully stolen billions of dollars from both individuals and businesses during that time. They come in various forms. Some are the lone-wolf type and operate on their own with the sole purpose of intruding into networks for their own personal financial gain. Others operate in small groups of like-minded hackers. There are also large and sophisticated organized-crime rings with significant financial backing to carry out their crimes. Many of these rings operate in Russia and parts of Eastern Europe. Most criminal hackers, whether lone wolf or part of a larger criminal ring, will steal money directly via wire fraud or steal sensitive data, including personally identifiable information, payment cards, or intellectual property that they can later sell on the black market.

Nation-State Actors

These attackers are those who are funded, trained, and directed by governments to carry out their attacks. They have the most resources of any hacker group profile and are therefore the most powerful. They started appearing in the past ten years and made headlines as both businesses and the US government accused specific foreign governments of being directly involved in some of the highest-profile attacks against them. Many of these attacks involved the exfiltration of highly sensitive personally identifiable information and protected health information, espionage, and intellectual property theft. They often use highly customized and advanced attack codes and are excellent at covering their digital footprints. To do this, they often leverage the latest in kernel-level rootkits, stenography, and encryption methods. Many experts believe that, unlike the criminal hackers we were used to seeing, the nation-state actors may have additional motives besides financial gain, since many of these attacks were aimed at both the private and the public sector. By obtaining the personally identifiable information of government officials, there could be a more sinister plot playing out involving extortion of people in power. To make matters worse, nation-state hackers serve as teachers to lower-level hackers, who will work to copy their techniques.

Hacktivists

This attacker often follows the mantra that information should be free and available to all. They are usually motivated by politics. They are activists who carry out attacks to make their message clear to a particular organization they disagree with. The Internet has given this type of hacker a broad platform upon which to get his or her message to a very large audience that extends far beyond their victims. These groups can be very disorganized and may rely on only some basic attacking tools that are freely available and widely known. Others have become more sophisticated and more successful over time. Their goal is not financial gain but to embarrass their targets, which has come to be known in the hacker community as "doxing."

Rogue Employees and Malicious Insiders

Attacks by trusted employees and longtime vendors are some of the most difficult to prevent. Often, these are the people who have been given the keys to the data kingdom, with privileges to access highly confidential and valuable data. Those who work in or contract for the IT department, human resources, and research divisions and low-level support staff who work for high-level employees could all fit into this profile. They are often not very well funded, but they are armed with the knowledge of the inner workings of networks and the experience to navigate databases and have relationships with people who have access to valuable information. They may be difficult to spot, as they operate under the radar. Their motives, like those of other hackers, are often linked to financial gain. However, some are driven by emotions. They may have developed an ax to grind with management or feel the need to attack for a variety of other reasons related to a poor working relationship with their respective firms.

The TOR Network, a.k.a. the "Dark Web"

Soon after they have successfully exfiltrated data, many criminal attackers take part in a robust underground economy, where they buy, sell, and trade their stolen goods. What has become known as the onion router (commonly referred to as TOR) is a mysterious underworld, known to many as the "dark web." It plays host to a variety of other criminal activities, including illegal-drug dealing, child pornography exchange, and exchanges of tool kits used to carry out additional cybercrimes. It provides a largely anonymous market where identities of buyers and sellers are hidden, and sales tracking is almost impossible. It is not accessible via traditional browsers and requires downloading specific software before it can be accessed.

McAfee's recent study of the dark web, "The Hidden Data Economy," sheds light on the black-market value of various forms of stolen data originating in the United States, Canada, the United Kingdom, Australia, and the European Union. There are a number of factors that dictate the going rate. Below is a summary of McAfee's findings from their report.

Financial Data

Let's start with payment-card information. McAfee found a wide range of prices for payment cards. Random card numbers pulled from a hacked database of US cardholders were being sold for between $5 and $8 each. Those same cards across Canada, the United Kingdom, Australia, and the European Union ranged from $20 to $30. Values went up significantly when those card numbers were sold in combination with additional demographic information about the cardholder. Known in the dark web as "fullzinfo," this includes the cardholder's full name, billing address, payment-card number, CVV2 (the three-digit "card verification value" printed on the back of the card), expiration date, PIN, social security number, mother's maiden name, and date of birth. Fullzinfo was being sold for $30 each in the United States, $35 in the United Kingdom, $40 in both Canada and Australia, and $45 in the European Union. Fullzinfo may also contain username and login credentials, allowing the buyer to change mailing addresses.

There may also be variations of data elements being sold, which are often referred to as a "dump track one" or "dump track two." Dump track one is alphanumeric and contains the card owner's name and account number. Track two is numeric and contains the account number, expiration date, the CVV code, and discretionary institution. In addition, the payment card's available balance will also influence price. McAfee's study revealed that US dump track one and two cards with high available balances were being sold for $110 each. They were fetching $160 in the United Kingdom, $180 in Canada, $170 in Australia, and $190 in the European Union.

The image below is an actual offering of payment cards from the dark web:

We are offering top quality cards:

All our cards come with PINs and instructions. You can use them at any ATM worldwide.
Our cards are equiped with magnetic strip and chip.
Once you purchase, we will email you a Full Guide on how to safely cash out.

Us cards · available balance $2,500(minimum) and up to $5,000.
usage:
✓ ATM
✓ Stores
✓ Online

Eu cards - available balance 2,500 Euro(minimum) and up to 4,500 Euro.
usage:
✓ ATM
✓ Stores
✓ Online

American Express cards · available balance $6,000 (minimum) and up to $8,000.
usage:
✓ ATM
✓ Stores
✓ Online

Daily withdrawal limits (ATM limits)
US cards have a $700-$1000 daily withdrawal limit.
✓ no limit online or in stores

Online payment service account access information is another form of financial data being actively marketed on the dark web. These include bank-to-bank transfer access and banking login credentials. Unlike payment cards, the main driver of price for this information is account balance. Online payment service account balances of $400 to $1,000 were being sold for $20 to $50 each, while those with balances ranging from $5,000 to $8,000 were going for $200 to $300 each. McAfee pulled this ad to show how one banking login credential was being marketed:

pnc bank login - $22xx balance + info

Vendor	smoothhydra (5) (3.6 ★)
Price	Ƀ0.833 ($190)
Ships from	Worldwide
Escrow	No

Product description

This is a listing for a pnc bank login account with around $2200 in balance

- Have all details for login and I can transfer balance to your account if you want

Bank To Bank Transfer To Any Usa Bank

Bank To Bank Transfer To Any Uk Bank

Bank To Bank Transfer To Any Euro Country Bank

Amount To Pay For That Depend On Amount You Want To Transfer

- chat with me for know more details: (Yahoo Messenger : cvvsale.hacking)

Sellers anticipate that buyers may be suspicious of the validity of financial data being sold and have come up with various methods to assure the buyers that their stolen data is still valid. Some will advertise their products on YouTube to display a visual ad. Others may provide a free payment card as a test, while others provide a replacement card policy if the account balance is not as advertised. In addition, buyers often use social validation via online forum reviews to asssess the reputation of sellers.

Login Access

Login access is another popular item sold on the dark web. Types of login access can range from individual accounts to access to critical infrastructure. We have seen evidence of this as security expert Idan Aharoni demonstrated in his article "SCADA Systems Offered for Sale in the Underground Economy." SCADA, Supervisory Control and Data Acquisitions, are computer systems that control various equipment, often found in critical infrastructure. Aharoni uncovered what appeared to be access to a French hydroelectric generator that would presumably give the buyer control of its functions. Below is a screenshot provided by the seller:

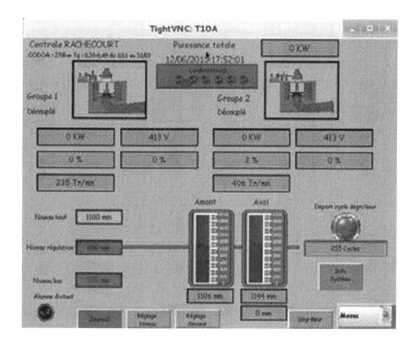

This is probably one of the most concerning trends we have seen in the underground data market. If access to critical infrastructure of the private sector is now available, where will the sellers go next? It is conceivable that criminal actors, nation-states, and well-funded terrorists are actively seeking access to the controls of power plants, financial markets, power grids, and satellites. They will have the means and the motives to purchase these credentials if the sellers can provide them. Once this information is obtained, some of the most dangerous criminals in the world might have the ability to cause significant harm across a large geographic area.

Online Services Access

In addition to financial information and access to physical controls, the dark web hosts access to various online services. These may include streaming movies, music, loyalty programs, and other digital services. These services are being sold for much less than financial information or access controls. The most expensive seems to be the $15 cost for an individual premium professional-sports streaming service. HBO NOW and HBO GO accounts were being sold for less than $10, as shown in the advertisement below:

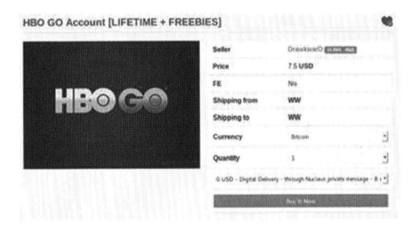

Access to free sites, such as those for hotel loyalty points are also in the market. McAfee highlighted a login credential sale to a hotel rewards account containing one hundred thousand points for a mere $20.

Online auction-site credentials, especially those of a person with excellent reviews, are a hot commodity on the dark web as well. Buyers who may want to carry out fraudulent sales activity on legitimate auction sites could pose as a seller with excellent reviews, luring unsuspecting buyers via their new auction-site identity.

Hacking as a Service

There is also a growing trend of selling hacking services on the dark web. Criminals can be hired to target specific companies and determine vulnerabilities. Some, as illustrated in the hacking service advertisement below, will offer refunds for failed attempts after a certain number of days.

(Source: http://icitech.org/wp-content/uploads/2016/09/ICIT-Brief-Deep-web-Exploitation-of-Health-Sector-Breach-Victims2.pdf.)

The trend of hacking as a service has allowed criminals with no technical skill to carry out criminal acts on the web.

Identities

The concept of identity theft is top of mind for many people today and literally keeping people awake at night. There is good reason to worry. According to a February 2016 report issued by the FTC:

- Tax- or wage-related ID theft is the most commonly reported type of identity theft. This type of fraud accounted for 45 percent of reported incidents. Payment-card fraud came in second at 16 percent.
- Some states have a higher per-capita rate of identity theft than others. Missouri, Connecticut, and Florida came in first, second, and third, respectively.
- In 2015 more than 490,000 identity theft–related complaints were made to the FTC. Identity theft is often discovered weeks or months after the initial crime is committed.
- Identity theft occurs in all age groups. In 2015 there were 20,905 complaints by victims under the age of nineteen and 26,305 by victims over seventy.
- Of all complaints made to the FTC, complaints for identity theft came in second, behind debt-collection complaints.

(Source: https://www.ftc.gov/system/files/documents/reports/consumer-sentinel-network-data-book-january-december-2015/160229csn-2015databook.pdf.)

A fascinating experiment conducted in 2015 by security firm Bitglass gave credibility to the FTC figures. The company created an Excel spreadsheet of fake names, social security numbers, credit-card numbers, addresses, and phone numbers. They watermarked the file so they could tell when and where it was opened by tracking IP addresses, geographic location, and device type. They posted it on the dark web, and within two weeks, it had been opened eleven hundred times in twenty-two countries. Bitglass concluded that crime rings in Russia and Nigeria were most likely involved in exchanging the data. (Source: https://techxplore.com/news/2015-04-bitglass-highlights-stolen-credit-card.html.)

W-2 Forms

Journalist Brian Krebs revealed a troubling trend of W-2 forms being marketed on the dark web. Krebs revealed the screenshot below from the dark web, advertising the sale of thirty-six hundred Florida residents' W-2 forms under the heading "W2 2016." The data elements included the taxpayer's employer name, employer ID, employer address, home address, social security number, and income information related to 2016 wages and taxes withheld. Each W-2 was being sold for between $4 and $20 in bitcoin. Presumably the buyer would use the data to steal tax refunds and commit additional identity theft.

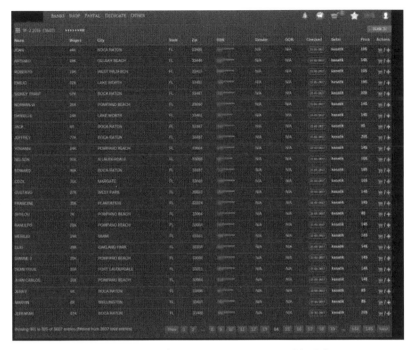

(Source: https://krebsonsecurity.com/2017/01/
shopping-for-w2s-tax-data-on-the-dark-web/.)

There is even further evidence of a very active marketplace for personally identifiable information on the dark web. McAfee demonstrates in the screenshot below how an online identity might be marketed. In this example, there are fourteen different data elements associated with one person. Right below that are several associated social media login credentials for the victim, including Facebook, Instagram, Google, YouTube, and others.

Armed with this information, a criminal could take over the entire digital life of a victim, This could cause significant financial harm, damage credit ratings, affect reputations, and take significant time to correct.

Medical Records

Medical records are also very valuable assets that are often bought and sold on the dark web. With this information, a drug addict could obtain prescription drugs. An illegal immigrant could access health care and obtain expensive medical devices. Moreover, medical records typically come with many other data elements to perpetuate additional identity theft. This explains the relatively high market value of a medical identity, which can fetch $60 per record. (Source: http://www.cnbc.com/2016/03/10/dark-web-is-fertile-ground-for-stolen-medical-records.html.)

According to a report by journalist Brian Krebs called "Day in the Life of a Stolen Healthcare Record," the market for medical identities is alive and well, as shown in the screenshot of a medical identity for sale below:

Mick Coady, a partner in the health information and security practice at PricewaterhouseCoopers, recently gave an interview to CNBC in which he revealed the black-market values for medical identities. According to Mr. Coady, a single medical record can sell for "up to $1,100" on the dark web. "About two years ago, it was probably worth no more than $50." (Source: http://www.cnbc.com/2016/03/09/as-health-data-breaches-increase-what-do-you-have-to-lose.html.)

Common Methods of Attack

Hackers use a variety of techniques to carry out their criminal acts. In this section we look to summarize some of the more common ways they do it. Surprisingly, some of these methods are very simple and low tech. Others were developed by highly skilled hackers and often made available for free in an easily executable software program. Others are advanced but made available to low-level hackers as pay-as-a-service hacks.

Website Attack Vectors

According to a 2016 study by the Security Engineering Research Team (SERT), website-application attacks are responsible for 24 percent of all online attacks as of the second quarter of 2016. Two of the most common types of website-application attacks are SQL injections (SQLi) and cross-site scripting. Organizations often fall victim to these attacks when application developers fail to protect and maintain their codes with proper application firewalls.

SQLi occurs when an attacker injects a malicious SQL statement into a form on a target website. This allows the attacker to siphon information from the company's database, which may include sensitive customer information and payment-card data.

Cross-site scripting occurs when the attacker exploits an existing web-application vulnerability. This allows hackers to push scripts and other information-stealing tools onto the pages of a victim's website.

Distributed Denial-of-Service Attacks (DDoS)

DDoS attacks occur when an attacker deliberately overloads a target server with an abnormal amount of traffic. Attackers often use an army of infected computers that they control, known as a "botnet," to carry out the information requests. This often results in a crashed server, knocking the target website off line, effectively disrupting normal business. As more and more common household devices become connected to the Internet, attackers are able to leverage an ever-growing army of devices to carry out these attacks.

For many of the victims, lost Internet traffic equates to lost revenues. According to a survey Dyn sponsored and published in August 2016, the majority of companies surveyed calculate that an Internet outage costs them a minimum of $1,000 per minute. (Source: http://dyn.com/blog/detecting-and-mitigating-a-cloud-outage-internet-performance-management-in-action/.)

In a cruel twist of fate, Dyn would become a victim of a cyberattack themselves just a few months later. We will discuss that incident in more detail later in this book.

In other studies, the average data center downtime is ninety-five minutes, causing an average loss of $740,000. However, if the outage is due to cybercrime or a DDoS attack, the costs increase to $981,000. Moreover, cyber-crime represents the fastest-growing cause of data center outages, rising from 2 percent of outages in 2010 to 18 percent in 2013 to 22 percent in 2015. (Source: https://www.ponemon.org/.)

Even more disconcerting is the fact that there is evidence of hacking groups providing DDoS services for very af-fordable fees. A crime group based in Russia that goes by the name Forceful provides DDoS services at the follow-ing rates:

- Daily: $60
- Weekly: $400
- 10 percent discount on orders of $500
- 15 percent discount on orders of $1,000

In addition, buyers can legally purchase "stressors" online. These are supposedly designed to test your own website for strength against various DDoS attacks. Pricing depends on the stressor's duration and bandwidth and ranges from $10 to $1,000 per day. (Source: https://www.symantec.com/connect/blogs/ddos-attacks-bigger-stronger-scarier.)

Ransomware

Ransomware incidents use a type of malicious code that encrypts the victim's data files, making them unusable. The hacker usually demands payment in return for recovering the data files. It is one of today's fastest-growing cyberthreats. FBI statistics reveal a disturbing trend. In 2014 their offices received more than eighteen hundred complaints regarding incidents that resulted in $23 million in losses to victims. In 2015, complaints rose to twenty-four hundred and losses to more than $24 million. In 2016 those numbers increased drastically. After the just the first quarter of 2016, the FBI announced that $209 million had been paid to ransomware hackers. That put us on pace to pay approximately $1 billion by the end of 2016. The eye-popping costs should not come as much of a surprise. Without access to their data, many businesses simply cannot function at all. They often elect to pay the ransom demand in lieu of the much greater financial burden of an extended business interruption.

We have seen various forms of ransomware evolve over recent years:

Fake antivirus apps: Criminals use applications to mislead users into believing their computer systems need repair. They request payment to remediate a problem that never existed.

Lockers: The device used to access files becomes infected with malware, preventing access to any data it holds. Once the malware is removed, the user regains access to all the data.

Crypto ransomware: Most often spread by spam e-mail, this method installs malware on a device or server and also encrypts individual files. Removal of the malware will not allow access to the files. A unique encryption key, known only to the criminal, is needed to decrypt the files. Ransom payment, typically in the form of a few thousand dollars in bitcoin, is usually demanded in exchange for the key.

Without the proper data backups, victims are often faced with the decision to pay the ransom without any guarantee that the hacker will release the decryption key. Fortunately, there is evidence that hackers do release the decryption key.

Here is a screenshot of what a victim of the common CryptoLocker ransomware might see. Here, the hackers not only demand payment, but they threaten to permanently hold the data hostage if payment is not made in a specified time period.

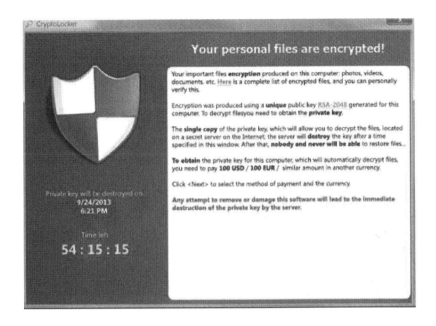

According to Symantec's "Ransomware and Businesses 2016" report, there is growing evidence that hackers are targeting specific businesses, as opposed to what were previously believed to be indiscriminate attacks. In addition, ransomware criminal groups are using more sophisticated attack techniques, displaying a level of expertise similar to that seen in many advanced cyberespionage attacks. The report's key findings were as follows:

- The services sector was targeted 38 percent of the time and was the most affected business sector.
- Manufacturing, considered by many as a lower-risk industry for cyberattacks, was hit with 17 percent of infections.

- The average ransom demand has more than doubled and is now $679, up from $294 at the end of 2015.
- The number of new variants of ransomware discovered has been steadily increasing since 2011. In 2015 one hundred new variant "families" were discovered.
- Paid ransomware services, known as ransomware-as-a-service (RaaS), expanded the number of cybercriminals who can acquire and use their own ransomware.
- The trend toward crypto-ransomware has continued. The vast majority of new ransomware variants discovered so far in 2016 are crypto-ransomware.
- Between January 2015 and April 2016, the United States was the region most affected by ransomware, with 28 percent of global infections. Canada, Australia, India, Japan, Italy, the UK, Germany, the Netherlands, and Malaysia also made the top ten.
- 43 percent of ransomware victims were employees of organizations.

Ransom payments may be only the first step in recovering from a ransomware attack. The victims must also determine whether or not the hackers accessed any sensitive information of other individuals that may trigger the legal obligation to notify them.

Social Engineering Fraud

Today's criminals have become masters at exploiting our natural tendencies to trust other people. This has given rise to one of the most common forms of attack, known as social engineering. Instead of hacking computers, they are essentially *hacking people*. It is usually carried out via e-mail but can also be done via phone calls, and these criminals have been highly successful. In fact, according to the FBI, from October 2013 to August 2015, more than eight thousand social-engineering victims from across the United States were defrauded of almost $800 million. The average loss amounted to $130,000. It is a problem that extends well beyond US borders. Law-enforcement officials have reported social-engineering crimes in seventy countries.

There are several types of social-engineering scams. Let's start with a review of the methods that involve some form of network penetration:

Phishing: This method is usually carried out in mass e-mail campaigns. It can be likened to a Hail Mary pass in a football game. The criminal has likely had no prior communication with the group and sends the e-mail along with a malware-laden attachment or link to a boo-by-trapped website that infects anyone who clicks on it. This can often provide a gateway into a network, allowing the attacker to access and exfiltrate data, control e-mail accounts, and harvest other credentials. Criminals have been very successful, as indicated by the "Verizon 2015 Data Breach Investigations Report." (Source: http://www.verizon.com/about/news/2015-data-breach-report-info/.) It revealed that 23 percent of those receiving a phishing e-mail opened it, and 11 percent clicked on the attachment or website link that came with it.

Spear phishing: This is similar to phishing, the main difference being the intended target. With spear phishing, the attacker is targeting a specific group of people who may have access to sensitive data or may be empowered to transfer funds. A common target group would be human resources or accounting departments.

Business executive fraud/whaling: With this method attackers target one high-level executive, such as a CEO. Once they penetrate the network, they may take over the CEO's e-mail account. Often, a request for a wire transfer or other sensitive information from the compromised e-mail account is made to someone responsible for processing transfers. The demand is often made in an urgent or time-sensitive manner. The one receiving the request typically responds to a CEO immediately, diligently following orders from the most powerful person in the organization.

Bogus invoice: Here, an attacker targets a business that has a long-standing relationship with a supplier. The supplier's network is compromised, and an e-mail account is taken over. The attacker might locate an invoice template and copy it, creating the bogus invoice. The attacker invoices the business and asks them to wire funds to make payment to an alternate, fraudulent bank account via e-mail. The e-mail request appears very similar to that from a legitimate account; it would take very close scrutiny to determine that it was fraudulent.

There are several low-tech forms of social-engineering scams.

Interactive voice response/phone phishing/"vishing": Here, an attacker will use a phone and his or her voice as the weapons of choice. Attackers will typically target employees with elevated privileges to transfer data or funds. They often use caller ID technology to make it appear to the victim that an incoming call is coming from a recognized company. They may also use automation to replicate a legitimate-sounding message that appears to come from a bank or other financial institution and directs the recipient to respond in order to "verify" confidential information.

Dumpster diving/forensic recovery: Here, a data thief might literally dive into a Dumpster or other trash receptacle to harvest sensitive information. Old computer equipment, printers, and paper files often contain this information.

Baiting: An attacker will often leave malware-infected removable media, such as USB drives, in a location where a curious employee may find it. When he or she attaches the USB to his or her own computer, criminals can inject malicious code to exfiltrate valuable data.

Tailgating: Criminals may gain unauthorized access to company premises by following closely behind an employee or security professional entering a facility. Even more brazen criminals might openly present themselves to a security guard as someone who has official business with the company.

Diversion: Deliberate attempts are made to misdirect a courier or transport company to reroute a package.

Now that we have a basic understanding of some of the more common methods of attack, it is important to gain insight into some popular tools of the trade used by hackers.

Here Is a Device That May Be Used to Hack Wi-Fi Networks

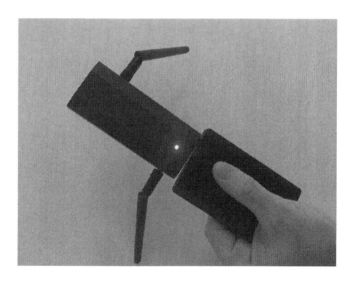

According to a 2016 report by Kaspersky Labs (http://www.infosecurity-magazine.com/news/kaspersky-lab-quarter-of-wi-fi/), one-quarter of all Wi-Fi hotspots around the world are unsecured and pose a significant threat to those using them. The report concluded that after analyzing thirty-one million Wi-Fi hotspots, 25 percent had no password or encryption protection. An additional 3 percent were using the outdated and easily cracked Wired Equivalent Privacy (WEP) to encrypt data. The remaining 72 percent were running the more secure Wi-Fi Protected Access (WPA) protocol. These are still vulnerable to hackers if an easily guessed password is used or if it is publicly available in a shared location such as a café, hotel, or airport.

Even the so-called "secure" Wi-Fi networks are being penetrated with easily accessed hacking tools. These are handheld devices that resemble a router and can be *bought legally* online for about $150. They were originally designed by security researchers with good intentions. They were designed to help investigators find unauthorized and perhaps malicious Wi-Fi networks that may have been set up and made accessible within a business's premises. Unfortunately, hackers have found a way to use this device for their own nefarious activities.

The device has two antennas. One finds an existing Wi-Fi network, and the other finds all the devices connected to that network. When activated, the device impersonates the legitimate Wi-Fi network, creating what appears to be an exact duplicate Wi-Fi with the same name. Typical users are unable to tell the difference. The device then disconnects every user who was originally connected to the legitimate Wi-Fi. As the users' devices automatically seek to reconnect, the hacker's device intercepts them and connects them to the hacker's personal Wi-Fi. The hacker now owns the users' devices. The hacker can then see all e-mails and documents and can even inject malicious code to exfiltrate any data from the users' phones, tablets, laptops, or whatever else they were using to connect to the Wi-Fi network.

Hacking Tools Disguised as USB Devices

Hackers have been very good at disguising some of their tools. This device looks exactly like any common USB data-storage device. However, when the case is peeled back, one will realize that this is something much more sinister than a USB. It is, in fact, a keystroke injection attack platform. What does this mean? When the attacker inserts it into any computer, the "USB" tells the device "I am a keyboard." Most operating systems will by default trust the device and accept what they believe is a keyboard. Once connected, the hacker can remotely download payloads and exfiltrate data to any other computer the hacker directs it to. It is a remarkably simple and effective tool. As long as the attacker has physical access to the target computers, they can easily be exploited with this device which can be legally bought online for about forty-five dollars.

"PoisonTap"

Samy Kamkar, a leading cybersecurity expert, developed a tool to demonstrate how seemingly secure networks can be compromised. Although similar to the USB device, this tool can be used by attackers to easily access a locked, password-protected computer. As pictured below, the device is simply connected via a USB cable to the victim's computer. The victim's computer trusts the device. It collects cookies to enable the attacker to bypass two-factor authentication and to take over the victim's online accounts.

(Source: http://securityaffairs.co/wordpress/53507/ hacking/poisontap-hacking-tool.html.)

"Juice Jacking"

For several years data thieves have been able to target public device-charging kiosks as an attack vector. Hackers can easily manufacture a wall charger with inexpensive hardware components. When an unsuspecting victim plugs a device into the wall charger, it could infect the device with malware, leading to exfiltration of any data contained on it.

The manufacturers of some phones and devices, including iPhone and android, have begun to implement security measures to prevent connection to juice jacking outlets when they are plugged into them. Juice jacking is not possible if a device is charged with the original AC adapter that was included with the device. There are also products available for the sole purpose of disallowing data connections to be passed over a USB cable.

Phone Number Spoofing Services

Vishing scams are often perpetrated by using phone number spoofing services. The attackers can alert telephone networks to make the receiver of a call believe that they are calling from a specific physical location when they are not. In the early 2000s, these services became available to the public at minimal cost. They were originally designed to protect the identities of people who may have been in harmful situations or simply to be used to carry out pranks. However, criminals soon realized they could use this service to perpetrate various crimes. Commons schemes involve impersonation of police, utility companies, and medical insurers in attempts to extort money or steal sensitive data.

Prewritten Hacking Programs

There are possibly hundreds, perhaps thousands, of hacking programs available on various hacking forums. Many are available free of charge and are most often used by "Script Kiddie" hackers. These are typically younger, less experienced hackers who take advantage of the sinister roadmaps made available by their more experienced hacking peers. Some of the more popular programs to emerge in recent years include WinNuke, Metasploit, Back Orifice, and NetBus.

- **WinNuke**: This program allows the hacker to carry out a remote denial-of-service attack. By overloading the target server, the program crashes the network. Fortunately, this program will not damage data on the hard drive, but any unsaved data will be lost.
- **Metasploit**: This program is used to test the vulnerability of computer systems and allows hackers to break into remote systems. Metasploit currently has more than 438 payloads. They include command shell, which allows the hacker to run scripts and/or make commands against the host; Meterpreter, which enables users to control the screen of a device and to browse, upload, and download files; and dynamic payloads, which give the hacker the ability to evade antivirus products by generating unique payloads.
- **Back Orifice**: This program is known for its ease of use. It allows the hacker to control multiple

computers from a remote location and is particularly difficult for the end user to detect.

- **NetBus**: This program allows for remote administration and is known to empower the hacker to log keystrokes, capture screens, launch programs, browse files, shut down systems, and open and close CD trays. One of the most infamous consequences of this program occurred when it was used to plant child pornography on the work computer of a law scholar at Lund University. Thousands of images were discovered by system administrators. It was assumed that he knowingly downloaded them, and as a result he lost his research position at the faculty. When the issue became public, he fled the country and had to seek professional medical care to cope with the stress. He was acquitted of criminal charges in 2004, when the court concluded that NetBus had been used to control his computer.

Shockingly, many of these devices can be purchased legally online. How can this be? Shouldn't law enforcement ban the sale of these harmful tools? These are excellent questions I often hear repeated. It would seem prudent to ban them if the tools were used solely for criminal activity. However, many of these devices were originally designed for other security purposes aimed at identifying and preventing cyberthreats. Hackers eventually exploited them for their own criminal intent. It remains to be seen whether law enforcement or consumer-protection agencies will begin to focus attention on this glaring problem.

CHAPTER 3

Privacy Laws and the Legal Landscape

Privacy law, like any other subset of laws, is the product of an evolutionary process. In this chapter, we look at where we stand today in five distinct regions: the United States, Canada, the European Union, Latin America, and Asia. Each of these regions has paid significant attention to privacy regulation, and their laws have undergone massive revisions in recent years in a race to keep up with emerging technologies and associated threats. You will see that each region has its own quirks, and some are more heavily regulated than others. Ultimately, international privacy law is aimed at organizations that collect personal information. It requires specific controls and actions on the part of the data collector. Understanding an organization's legal obligations for protecting the data and its duties to respond in the aftermath of a data breach is critical. Failure to comply with a county's data-protection laws could result in significant financial and reputational harm. These laws will continue to evolve, so understand that what one is required to do today could change drastically tomorrow. It is highly recommended that any organization retain the services of an experienced privacy attorney before trying to navigate this daunting and dynamic terrain.

United States

Businesses operating in the United States will find no shortage of privacy laws and regulatory requirements imposed upon them concerning data security. These rules have evolved rapidly and have made the United States a world leader in establishing a robust and complicated set of legal frameworks for business to comply with. Lawmakers' intention to protect data subjects from the emerging cyberthreats has, unfortunately, left businesses to sort through laws, rules, and regulations at the state and federal level. The compliance puzzle will change from business to business. The business sector, the types of data elements being held, and the state of residence of the data subject will all play a part.

In 2003, California led the way, mandating what data businesses can legally collect, how they must protect that data, and what actions they need to take should the data become compromised. Since that time, many other states have followed California's lead and created their own sets of standards. As of this writing, there are forty-seven states, plus DC, Puerto Rico, Guam, and the Virgin Islands, with their own data-protection laws, with several revising them every year. Many state statutes contain similar language, while others differ in vast ways. For example, some are very specific about the types of controls that must be in place, such as requiring written information-security plans and encryption levels, while others require "reasonable" controls. After a breach of personally identifiable information, several states require notice to affected individuals within a clearly defined time frame, such as thirty or ninety days, while others require notice "without unreasonable delay." This leaves businesses to wonder what exactly is "reasonable" in the eyes of the attorney general, who enforces the state laws. The content requirements of the notice letter vary from state to state. Some require a description of how the incident occurred, the date it occurred, what the organization is doing to help the affected individual, and what they are doing to make sure it doesn't happen again. Other states, like Massachusetts, specifically want very limited information in the notice letter. In certain circumstances, states will require "substitute notice" describing a network-security breach on a company's website. The notice must be conspicuous and is generally expected to be posted for a period of ninety days. The definition of "personally identifiable information" can be narrow or very broad. The more data elements that a state brings under the definition of "personally identifiable information," the more likely an incident will trigger notice requirements in the aftermath of a network-security incident. For example, California has expanded its definition to include e-mail addresses in combination with usernames. Oregon revised its statute to include biometric data. It should be noted that the state of residence of the affected individual will trigger the specific state notice law. When a data breach involves individuals across multiple states, businesses must comply with every one of the state requirements, making compliance no easy task. In addition, many states, such as Washington and Rhode Island, are now requiring the notice letters to be sent to their attorneys general when there is data compromise of more than five hundred records.

There is some good news for businesses in some states. Tennessee has extended safe-harbor protections for incidents involving encrypted data. Illinois has extended safe harbor to HIPAA-compliant entities. Connecticut has clarified the time frame within which it expects its state residents to be notified and given businesses ninety days' time to notify, which is more than the more common thirty or forty-five days demanded by many state attorneys general.

The patchwork of notification laws that a business must comply with has led many to wonder if there is any hope for one standard, federal notification law to streamline compliance. Unfortunately, state attorneys general are resistant to that idea. In fact, on July 15, 2015, forty-seven state attorneys general wrote to Congress stating their case for maintaining their authority to implement and revise their cybersecurity and post-breach notification requirements. Therefore, it is safe to say that for the foreseeable future, businesses will need to keep a close eye on current statutory requirements and expect continued revisions in law from state to state, year over year.

If a data breach is large enough or affects a specific industry, there are several federal statutes and industry-specific mandates that businesses will also need to grapple with on top of those imposed by individual states. These can include HIPAA, GLB, FACTA, COPPA, and PCI-DSS. These are enforced by a wide array of regulatory authorities and often involve the Office of Civil Rights, the Federal Trade Commission, the Federal Communications Commission, the Consumer Finance Protection Board, and the Securities and Exchange Commission. We will go into these in more detail later in this book as we take a deeper dive into industry-specific risks.

Canada

Canada has a series of privacy statutes that are applied at federal, provincial, and territorial levels. Like those of other countries, Canadian statutes are focused on safeguarding personal information in the private, public, and health sectors. Federal government departments and agencies are governed by the regulations as outlined in the Privacy Act. The private sector must comply with four specific privacy statutes: the federal Personal Information Protection and Electronic Documents Act (PIPEDA), Alberta's Personal Information Protection Act (PIPA), British Columbia's Personal Information Act, and Quebec's Act

Respecting the Protection of Personal Information in the Private Sector. Specific provinces, such as Ontario, New Brunswick, Newfoundland, and Labrador, have passed legislation specific to protecting an individual's health-care information.

As in other countries, we have seen Canada's privacy laws evolve over time. In 2010, Alberta amended PIPA to require organizations to notify Alberta's Information and Privacy Commissioner of data-breach incidents under certain circumstances. These changes also empowered the privacy commissioner to require the organization to formally notify individuals who face a "real risk of significant harm" as a result of the data breach.

In 2015 there was a major revision of PIPEDA when Canada passed the Digital Privacy Act. The Digital Privacy Act expanded the data-breach notification requirement that was already in place in Alberta. The key components are:

Mandatory Notice Requirement
Notice—to Whom:

- Individuals, except where prohibited by law
- If notice is given to individuals, notice must be given to other organizations and government (a) if notifying organization believes it may reduce risk or mitigate harm or (b) in prescribed circumstances.

- Commissioner in prescribed form and manner where there is "real risk of significant harm"

Notice—When and How:

- Individuals and other organizations. Report to commissioner must be given "as soon as feasible" after it is determined that a breach occurred.
- Notice must be conspicuous and direct in the prescribed form and manner, except where indirect notice is prescribed.

Notice must contain

- sufficient information to allow an individual to understand the significance of the breach to them, and to take steps, if possible, to reduce the risk of harm or mitigate it; and
- any other prescribed information.

Heightened consent: Prior to the Digital Privacy Act, PIPEDA contained specific requirements concerning an individual's consent prior to collection or sharing of their personal data. The Digital Privacy Act has expanded this to require organizations to tell individuals about the information they collect, how it is used, and to whom it is disclosed. There are specific mandates for children and other vulnerable individuals. There are, however, exceptions to consent requirements when managing employees, fraud investigations, work product information, and certain business transactions.

Mandatory record keeping: Organizations are required to maintain a record of every breach of their controls where personal information is affected. The record-keeping requirement applies to all breaches, irrespective of whether or not there was a "real risk of significant harm." Should the commissioner request a copy of these records, the organization is compelled to comply with the request. Further, these records could pose challenges if requested by others. Plaintiffs' attorneys might request copies during litigation. Cyber insurance underwriters might request copies when assessing risk and determining insurance premiums.

Enforcement and penalties: Knowing violations of breach reporting or mandatory record-keeping requirements may result in fines ranging from $10,000 to $100,000. There is now an option of entering into a "compliance agreement" with the commissioner in court; however, careful consideration should be given prior to entering into one. On the one hand, these provide a limited form of "safe harbor," since they prevent the commissioner from bringing the matter before a federal court. On the other hand, they will not prohibit individuals or their attorneys from pursuing their complaints in federal court.

Commissioner publication: The commissioner reserves the right to publish any information disclosed via mandatory breach reporting or record-keeping disclosure.

European Union

Historically, the European Union regulated privacy via a series of fragmented policies among its member countries. However, in recent years it has started to compile a more consistent strategy in addressing data-privacy concerns. In February of 2013, the European Commission formally introduced five priorities: achieving cyber resilience, drastically reducing cybercrime, developing cyber defense policy and capabilities, developing the industrial and technological resources for cybersecurity, and establishing a coherent international cyberspace policy for the European Union and promotion of its core values. This ultimately led to the formation of the Network and Information Security (NIS) Directive.

Then, on May 4, 2016, the European Union announced sweeping changes to their privacy regulations with the passage of the General Data Protection Regulation (GDPR). The regulation is notable for both its size and scope. It requires organizations to implement a complex privacy-management system as a key component of their information and cybersecurity-management system. It provides for a consistent set of rules for all member states to follow and eliminates any inconsistencies that existed in prior regulation.

The key provisions of the GDPR include the following:

- **Geography**: It applies far beyond businesses operating in EU member countries. It also applies "to the processing of personal data of data subjects who are in the Union by a controller or processor not established in the Union, where the processing activities are related to: (a) the offering of goods or services, irrespective of whether a payment of the data subject is required, to such data subjects in the Union; or (b) the monitoring of their behavior as far as their behavior takes place within the Union."

What this means is that *any* company, regardless of geographic location, that collects, stores, or processes an EU resident's personal information is subject to these regulations.

- **Consent**: This requires data controllers to demonstrate that they obtained "clear affirmative action" on behalf of the data subject before collecting his or her information. Consent must always be given explicitly and should never be assumed. Reliance on prechecked boxes, silence, or no activity would be considered a violation of the consent provision.

- **Profiling**: There are restrictions on targeted advertising. An organization is prohibited from making decisions "based solely on automated processing, including profiling, which produces legal effects concerning [a data subject] or similarly significantly affects [a data subject]."

- **Procedural documentation**: Documentation of data-collection and processing activities is now required. Compliance must be demonstrated through implementing "appropriate technical and organizational measures."

- **Appoint a data-protection officer**: Organizations with more than 250 full-time employees are required to appoint a data-protection officer. Before engaging in risky data-processing activities, the data-protection officer is required to conduct a formal data-protection impact assessment.
- **Implement privacy by design**: Organizations are now required to undertake data-privacy impact assessment in the event that the relevant processing operation is "likely to result in high risk to the rights and freedoms of natural persons."
- **Mandatory data-breach reporting**: Organizations are required to notify data subjects when a data breach is "likely to result in a high risk to the rights and freedoms of natural persons." Of particular concern is the strict time requirement to notify the data subject within seventy-two hours of becoming aware of the incident. We will discuss some of these challenges later in this book.
- **Right to erasure**: Data subjects have enhanced rights, including the "right to be forgotten," which will force companies to take steps to minimize or eliminate the data subjects' digital footprint.
- **Penalties**: Organizations need to better understand not only the risks associated with the new regulations but also the bottom-line consequences for noncompliance. There are significant increases

in the size of penalties for those who fail to comply. All EU countries will impose the same fines—€20 million or four percent of worldwide annual revenue, whichever is greater.

There is a two-year implementation period, which allows EU member states time to comply with the new privacy rules. Given what is required to comply, some companies will need every bit of the two years to get their respective houses in order.

One way to start would be to consider joining the Privacy Shield Framework. This program was designed by the US Department of Commerce and European Commission with the goal of providing both US and EU member companies with a vehicle for compliance with EU data-protection requirements when transferring personal data from the European Union to the United States. Companies interested in joining will need to review the minimum required standards in their entirety. There is a self-certification process through the Department of Commerce, which requires a public commitment to comply with the framework's requirements. While joining is voluntary, members will be held accountable to these standards under enforceable US law. Prospective members can obtain additional information at https://www.privacyshield.gov/Key-New-Requirements and https://www.privacyshield.gov/article?id=Privacy-Policy-FAQs-1-6.

Latin America

Latin American privacy law has evolved to protect individuals from unfair practices by private sector companies and instituted protections from unreasonable government intrusion into their private lives. Thirteen jurisdictions in Latin America now have comprehensive privacy laws: Argentina, Aruba, Bahamas, Chile, Colombia, Costa Rica, Curaçao, Dominican Republic, Mexico, Nicaragua, Peru, Trinidad and Tobago, and Uruguay. There are some distinct differences in privacy laws among countries, but there are common themes baked into the laws of all Latin American member countries:

- **Notice**: Latin American privacy laws require that proper notice be given to individuals with respect to what personal information is collected, why it is collected, and with whom it is shared.
- **Choice**: Every privacy law has some form of individual affirmative choice. Levels and types of consent vary from country to country.
- **Security**: These laws also require that companies implement reasonable controls to protect that information from loss; misuse; and unauthorized access, disclosure, alteration, and destruction.
- **Access and correction**: Individuals have the right to access the information that organizations have collected about them. If possible, they are granted the opportunity to correct, update, or suppress that information to some extent. Most countries in Latin

America require organizations to respond to access and correction requests in a much shorter period of time than other countries around the world.

- **Data integrity**: Organizations must ensure that their records are accurate, complete, and kept up to date for the purposes for which the information will be used.
- **Data retention**: Personal information should be retained only for the time required to achieve the original purpose of the processing. Some laws mandate specific retention periods, while others set limits on how long data may be retained by an organization after the purpose of use has been achieved.

(Source: https://iapp.org/news/a/data-protection-laws-in-latin-america-an-overview/.)

Asia

Asia's privacy protections evolved with laws passed in 1988; 1995; and 2005, when the Asia-Pacific Economic Cooperation (APEC) agreed on their privacy framework. The APEC privacy framework sets forth a set of principles for collecting, processing, and transferring personal data. Its main requirement is that personal data should be collected fairly with the data subject's voluntary, informed consent. Once it is collected, the data should be processed securely in accordance with the purposes for which it has been collected. While the privacy framework does not require data-breach notification to regulators of affected individuals, some member countries have enacted these requirements. India, the Philippines, South Korea, and Taiwan have all enacted mandatory data-breach notification requirements. Japan and China have industry sector–specific breach-notification regulations. Voluntary but strongly encouraged data-breach notification laws exist in Hong Kong and Singapore.

Hong Kong's Cyber Fortification Initiative (CFI): Hong Kong's banking regulator, the Monetary Authority (HKMA), began to focus on cybersecurity issues with the issuance of the Cyber Fortification Initiative in 2016. Its main components are:

- **The Cyber Resilience Assessment Framework**: This is a self-assessment tool to give organizations insight into their vulnerabilities. It will provide benchmarking data and cyber-attack simulation testing based on real-time cyber threat intelligence.
- **The Professional Development Program**: The HKMA is collaborating with the Hong Kong Applied Science and Technology Research Institute and the Hong Kong Institute of Bankers to develop a program aimed at increasing the number of cybersecurity professionals.
- **The Cyber Intelligence Sharing Platform**: The HKMA will work with the Hong Kong Association of Banks to promote cyber threat intelligence sharing.

It is reasonable to expect that clearer standards for cyber-security-threat identification, risk management, and incident response will emerge in the coming months. Hong Kong's financial-services sector has taken the lead, and their response will likely serve as a roadmap for other industries and influence other regions in Asia.

CHAPTER 4

Industry-Specific Risks

Cyber risk is industry agnostic. Criminals will attack companies in any industry, of any size, and anywhere in the world. If you are online, you are subject to an attack. That said, financially motivated hackers tend to focus on specific industries that might have larger amounts of valuable digital assets that can be monetized. For this reason I decided to highlight five distinct industries that tend to attract hackers: health care, retail, transportation, manufacturing, and utilities.

Health Care

The health-care industry has battled data thieves for years, and it has struggled mightily in the fight. Three things have worked against them. First, the Health Insurance Portability and Accountability Act (HIPAA) regulated the industry in such a way as to define exactly how organizations are to protect data. It has evolved as technology evolved to reflect updated standards to protect electronic health records. Detailed requirements for protecting patient data must be complied with. Second, many health-care organizations struggle with shrinking budgets. In fact, most spend only about 10 percent of their total IT budgets on cybersecurity. Third, as we stated earlier in this book, protected health information (PHI) commands a high price on the black market, making it a highly sought-after data asset.

HIPAA applies to both "covered entities" and "business associates." Covered entities generally include health-care providers, health insurers, health-care clearinghouses, and employer-sponsored health plans. A business associate is generally defined as a person or entity that performs certain functions involving the use or disclosure of protected health information on behalf of a covered entity. The roles and responsibilities of the covered entity and its business associates are written in a business associate agreement.

There are four areas of HIPAA that any covered entity or business associate should be familiar with:

- The privacy rule, which creates data-security standards and the required safeguards to protect all forms of PHI.

- The security rule, which provides the detailed requirements to meet compliance and focuses on electronic PHI. It requires implementing physical, administrative, and technical safeguards.
- The enforcement rule, which outlines the procedures to be followed regarding hearings and penalties.
- The breach-notification rule, which explains the requirements to comply with notifying both the US Department of Health and Human Services (HHS) and affected individuals when PHI is accessed by an unauthorized party.

It is expected that organizations will conduct a formal risk assessment to measure compliance with HIPAA standards and to use it as a means to identify gaps and remediate vulnerabilities.

The HHS Office of Civil Rights (OCR) will investigate incidents involving unauthorized disclosures of PHI, enforce compliance, and issue fines. If a covered entity or business associate is deemed noncompliant, the OCR will resolve the issue in one of three ways:

- The entity agrees to voluntary compliance.
- The OCR demands corrective action.
- The OCR negotiates a resolution agreement.

There is a tiered penalty structure as outlined below:

HIPAA Violation	Minimum Penalty	Maximum Penalty
Unknowing	$100 per violation, with an annual maximum of $25,000 for repeat violations (Note: maximum that can be imposed by State Attorneys General regardless of the type of violation)	$50,000 per violation, with an annual maximum of $1.5 million
Reasonable Cause	$1,000 per violation, with an annual maximum of $100,000 for repeat violations	$50,000 per violation, with an annual maximum of $1.5 million
Willful neglect but violation is corrected within the required time period	$10,000 per violation, with an annual maximum of $250,000 for repeat violations	$50,000 per violation, with an annual maximum of $1.5 million
Willful neglect and is not corrected within required time period	$50,000 per violation, with an annual maximum of $1.5 million	$50,000 per violation, with an annual maximum of $1.5 million

(source:https://www.ama-assn.org/practice-management/
hipaa-violations-enforcement).

Criminal Penalties

The Department of Justice handles incidents in which criminal activity is suspected. Offenses committed under false pretenses allow penalties to be increased to $100,000, with up to five years in prison. Incidents involving the intent to sell; transfer; or use PHI for commercial advantage, personal gain, or malicious harm can lead to fines of $250,000 and imprisonment up to ten years.

Audits

In 2015 the OCR announced that it would commence audits of 350 covered entities and 50 business associates. Those selected will be subject to either a remote or on-site audit of compliance with HIPAA standards. They will be given only two weeks to respond to data requests. Any data provided after the two-week deadline will not be accepted. If compliance issues are identified, the covered entity or business associate may be subject to an additional on-site audit and possible enforcement action.

The OCR will focus on

- security risk analysis practices;
- breach notification;
- notice of privacy practices;
- individual access to PHI;
- security device and media controls;
- data transmission;
- encryption and decryption;
- physical controls; and
- workforce training.

For additional information on the audit protocols, refer to the HHS website: http://www.hhs.gov/ocr/privacy/hipaa/enforcement/audit/protocol.html.

Retail

In 2006 representatives of the major card brands formed the PCI Security Standards Council to protect consumers by developing global data-security standards. There are twelve basic data-security standards that include approximately 250 sub-requirements, which are known as PCI data-security standards. These apply to merchants and credit-card processors that store, process, or transmit cardholder data.

Despite these mandates, retailers of all sizes have fallen victim to payment-card theft. It is a significant problem within the United States, where almost half the world's credit-card fraud takes place. To combat that trend, new technology has been adopted in the form of "chip and pin" credit cards. These payments cards are referred to as EMV cards, which stands for Europay, Mastercard and Visa.This method of payment has been adopted in Canada and Europe and has proven effective in combating the threat posed by cybercriminals. This was a significant change from the traditional method of swiping credit cards through a device that reads cardholder data via a magnetic stripe. Now, payment cards equipped with EMV technology contain a chip containing dynamic authentication information that changes with each transaction. Customers can then enter a PIN.

Merchants will be able to accept payment three ways, each method having varying degrees of security:

- Most Secure: Customer inserts the EMV card and enters his or her PIN.
- Less Secure: Customer inserts the EMV card and signs the receipt.
- Least Secure: Customer swipes the EMV card and signs the receipt, just as he or she always did, since the new EMV cards can still be used on the traditional swiping terminals.

In order to take advantage of the new and more secure method of payment, issuing banks will need to provide the new cards to their customers, and merchants will need to upgrade their payment terminals.

This is where the "liability shift," effective October 1, 2015, came into play between the card-issuing bank and the merchant. Consider these two scenarios:

- The bank issues the new chip and PIN credit cards to customers. The merchant does not upgrade its traditional magnetic swipe terminals to accept the new cards. The new cards are used at the merchant store. The merchant is breached by hackers, and counterfeit cards are created and used. *The liability for counterfeit-card transactions will shift to the merchant.*
- The bank issues only the traditional magnetic stripe cards. The merchant upgrades its terminals to accept the new chip and PIN cards. The magnetic stripe

cards are used at the merchant's store. The merchant is breached by hackers, and counterfeit cards are created and used. *The liability for counterfeit-card transactions will fall back on the bank.*

It should be noted that the new EMV technology will not prevent credit-card fraud for online shopping or any other time a credit card is not physically present for a transaction. In fact, the new technology may drive hackers to focus even more, if not exclusively, on online transactions. This narrowed focus of hackers to the online world, coupled with the fact that the volume of online sales hit new records in November and December 2016, as shoppers spent an amazing $91.7 billion during that two-month span, leads to an ominous conclusion. This trend has created fertile grounds for hackers, so online retailers beware.

Navigating a Retail Hack

There are specific challenges that retailers will need to confront in the aftermath of a successful cyberattack against their networks. Each card brand will have a specific set of requirements that retailers must follow in the immediate aftermath of a data-security incident in which payment cards may have been compromised. In many cases, the bank that issues credit cards will notify the merchant that a number of defrauded cardholders shopped at its store. The banks conclude that a specific retailer was the common point of purchase for a number of cardholder victims and likely was the source of cardholder theft.

The card brands may then assign their own forensic investigator, referred to as a PFI, to investigate the matter. Unfortunately for the retailer, these investigations can become unilateral and may not address some key factors that will ultimately place the retailer in a negative position, require remediation, and lead to monetary fines. It is therefore crucial that a retailer hire its own forensic investigator to conduct an independent investigation.

The hiring should be done by the retailer's attorney to protect attorney-client privilege, should litigation arise in the future. The retailer's investigator should have a healthy dialogue with the PFI and take the opportunity to negotiate any negative findings unfairly attributed to the retailer. This negotiation should be done *prior* to the PFI issuing his or her final report, since it is extremely rare for a PFI to reverse any final report conclusions.

A very important point to be addressed is the window of intrusion. This is the period from the time the hackers first accessed the network to the time they left. This time frame is important, since it will have a direct impact on the costs that the hacked retailer may be ultimately responsible for. The window of intrusion may determine the number of payment cards that will need to be reissued, the amount of fraud that will be suspected as a result of the hack, and the number of people who need to be notified. If the retailer has significant transaction volume, different windows of intrusion could result in a difference of thousands or even millions of dollars in costs.

PCI Fines

After the PFI completes the final report, he or she may find noncompliance with certain PCI data-security standards. This may ultimately lead to fines and fees levied against the retailer. Most fines fall below $100,000. The PCI is typically given the authority to impose fines based on written service agreements between merchant banks and merchants. Fines are typically not levied until at least thirty days after the final report is issued, so remediation within that time period may help reduce or prevent a fine. Retailers should note that fines may be levied on a monthly basis until remediation is complete, so making this a priority is extremely important.

It would be prudent for a retailer to engage a qualified security assessor (QSA) to assist in PCI compliance matters. QSAs can perform audits and consult with retailers to identify any noncompliance with PCI data-security standards and can make recommendations for remediation.

Transportation

Operator errors, driving under the influence, and product defects have long been blamed for catastrophic accidents in the transportation industry. However, recent headlines revealed how cyber risk has emerged as a new and disturbing threat to airlines, railway companies, auto manufacturers, and ocean cargo carriers.

Those in the transportation sector have embraced the Internet of Things and transformed what were once far-reaching concepts into some of the most common components of the cars and planes they manufacture. They often rely on a secure Internet connection to function safely and efficiently. Recent headlines, however, raised concern and started a debate: Can the transportation sector be hacked? If so, what are the consequences?

Automobiles

In July 2015, Fiat Chrysler announced a recall of 1.4 million vehicles after white hat hackers demonstrated that they could take control of a Jeep Cherokee's braking system, change vehicle speed, and affect operation of the transmission, air conditioning, and radio controls. Hackers gained remote access by exploiting a software vulnerability in the vehicle's Uconnect entertainment system. (Source: http://www.theguardian.com/business/2015/jul/24/fiat-chrysler-recall-jeep-hacking.)

The stakes have been raised even higher with recent advances in the development of driverless cars, as more vehicles will become completely reliant on secure technology. Safety concerns were raised after a series of crashes allegedly caused by the failures of Tesla's autopilot technology, resulting in the death of a passenger. This prompted Tesla to announce efforts to improve its autopilot software, including "advanced processing of radar signals."

The Department of Transportation has also recognized the risks associated with technology. In January of 2016, the department entered into an agreement with seventeen major automakers to enhance driver safety, including information sharing to prevent cyberattacks on vehicles. According to the agreement, the National Highway Traffic Safety Administration will propose industry guidance for safe operation for fully autonomous vehicles. (Source: http://www.nhtsa.gov/About+NHTSA/Press+Releases/dot-initiatives-accelerating-vehicle-safety-innovations-01142016.)

Planes

Boeing recently became the subject of a hacker demonstration when a security researcher was able to access the entertainment systems of one of its planes in midflight. Boeing was adamant that the hacker could not have gained access to the aircraft's critical functions due to segregation of the two networks. However, the incident raised concerns throughout the airline industry, and an FBI investigation followed. (Source: http://www.wired.com/2015/05/possible-passengers-hack-commercial-aircraft/.)

Railway Systems

German security researchers SCADA Strangelove demonstrated, without naming the rail systems in question, that they, too, are vulnerable. Their December 2015 report highlighted vulnerabilities related to outdated software, default passwords, and lack of authentication. Moreover, entertainment and engineering systems were operating on the same network, leading to speculation that if one system was compromised, hackers could gain access to the other. Since rail switches are automated and dependent on properly operating networks, the theory of a system compromise leading to a head-on collision with another train was explored in the report. (Source: http://www.popsci.com/european-trains-vulnerable-to-hacking.)

Marine Shipping

An investigation by Verizon RISK concluded that modern-day pirates are increasingly relying on network intrusions as means to carry out crimes on the high seas. Verizon concluded that an unnamed shipping company's networks were penetrated by hackers, giving them precise information on which ships were carrying the most valuable contents. Hackers were then able to target their attacks on specific vessels, using bar codes to focus on individual shipping containers. (Source: http://www.digitaltrends.com/computing/tech-savvy-pirates/.) Hackers may also attempt to interfere with a ship's global positioning systems by transmitting false GPS signals to divert them to unintended destinations, where criminals may be lurking.

Thankfully, as of this writing, we have not seen any incidents of bodily injury or loss of life in the transportation sector directly attributed to a deliberate network compromise. Yet the findings of various researchers across multiple transportation sectors have led to some alarming conclusions. Law enforcement and transportation-safety regulators have taken these findings seriously and conducted investigations of their own. We can therefore expect with some degree of certainty that the transportation sector may be held to higher cybersecurity standards and will see the increased regulatory scrutiny that has been witnessed in other industries, such as health care and financial services. When networks containing sensitive data may be compromised, regulators who oversee that industry often propose protection standards that ultimately become mandates. Failure to comply often leads to lawsuits, settlements, fines, and significant reputational harm.

Until then, the transportation sector can start by following the best practices as outlined in the National Highway Traffic Safety Administration's "A Summary of Cybersecurity Best Practices," published in October 2014. Key observations and recommendations contained in the report include the following:

- Cybersecurity is a life-cycle process that includes elements of assessment, design, implementation, and operations, as well as an effective testing and certification program.
- The aviation industry has many parallels to the automotive industry in the area of cybersecurity.

- Strong leadership from the federal government could help the development of industry-specific cybersecurity standards, guidelines, and best practices.
- Ongoing shared learning with other federal government agencies is beneficial.
- Use of the National Institute of Standards and Technology (NIST) cybersecurity standards as a baseline is a way to accelerate the development of industry-specific cybersecurity guidelines.
- International cybersecurity efforts are a key source of information.
- Consider developing a cybersecurity simulator. It could facilitate identification of vulnerabilities and risk-mitigation strategies and can be used for collaborative learning (government, academia, private sector, and international).
- Cybersecurity standards for the entire supply chain are important.
- Foster industry cybersecurity groups for exchange of cybersecurity information.
- Use professional capacity building to address and develop cybersecurity skill sets, system designers, and engineers.
- Connected vehicle security should be end to end; vehicles, infrastructure, and V2X communication should all be secure.

The transportation sector is yet another industry that must learn to adapt to the systemic nature of cyber risk.

Through its ever-increasing reliance on evolving technology, cyber risk will certainly begin to move toward the top of the list of transportation-safety concerns. The captains of this industry can no longer claim ignorance of cybersecurity issues or completely delegate responsibility. They owe a duty to safeguard the flow of information exchange that effectively keeps our planes airborne and our cars on the road. Failure to do so could be catastrophic.

Financial Services

The financial-services industry has long been one of the most regulated industries in the United States. A dizzying array of regulators and laws can pose major challenges to the best of compliance officers. The emergence of cyber risk as more financial transactions occur online and the adoption of mobile banking technologies have only made matters worse. To summarize the rules and requirements, the SANS Institute issued a report called "Understanding Security Regulations in the Financial Services Industry." (Source: https://www.sans.org/reading-room/whitepapers/analyst/understanding-security-regulations-financial-services-industry-37027.) It summarizes a collective of controls required by the Gramm-Leach-Bliley Act (GLBA), the Dodd-Frank Wall Street Reform and Consumer Protection Act, and the Sarbanes-Oxley Act (SOX), and regulators including the Federal Trade Commission (FTC) and the Consumer Financial Protection Bureau (CFPB), as well as requirements mandated by payment-card industry data-security standards (PCI DSS).

Summary of controls:

- Establish and maintain an inventory of systems and applications containing and processing critical information.
- Establish regular periodic scanning.
- Scan applications regularly for vulnerabilities.
- Establish criteria for the prioritization of vulnerabilities and remediation activities.
- Pay special attention to internally or custom-developed applications with dynamic and static analyses.
- Establish secure coding as a culture, and provide qualified training on secure coding.
- Establish and document a secure development lifecycle approach that fits your business and developers.
- Combine functional testing and security testing of applications; assess for operational bugs and coding errors.
- Establish and enforce secure coding practices, such as pair programming and code review.
- Establish and enforce segregated development, testing, and production environments.
- Conduct periodic threat-modeling activities for all critical applications. Outcomes should inform information-security monitoring and fraud-detection activities.
- Perform regular application-penetration testing, and inform the regular vulnerability-scanning process to provide ongoing regression testing of applications.

- Establish and maintain policies and procedures.
- Continuously improve your visibility, assessment, and security programs.
- Periodically audit the controls structure, seeking to validate the effectiveness of the risk management activities listed above and of the controls themselves.

The regulation does not end at the federal level. As cyber threats become more common, mandates are beginning to form at the state level. In December 2016 the New York State Department of Financial Services (NYDFS) announced formal cybersecurity requirements for banks, insurance companies, and other financial-services companies. The new regulations will apply to approximately three thousand financial institutions, including banks, insurance companies, and other institutions operating under a license or authorization of New York state law, with certain exemptions. The web of regulation will not only ensnare large banks and insurance companies but also a long list of small businesses, including bail-bond agents, budget planners, charitable foundations, check cashers, holding companies, investment companies, and money transmitters.

The new regulations will require these organizations and entities to

- establish a cybersecurity program;
- adopt a written cybersecurity policy;

- designate a chief information-security officer or similar individual, responsible for implementing, overseeing, and enforcing its new program and policy;
- create a vendor-management program to ensure the security of their information systems;
- establish an incident-response plan to respond to and recover from a cybersecurity event; and
- implement a variety of additional controls, including annual penetration testing, multifactor authentication procedures, encryption standards, data-access limitations, formal log audit programs, and data-destruction processes.

A complete copy of the new rules can be found here: http://www.dfs.ny.gov/about/press/pr1612281.htm.

New York has traditionally led the way in regulating the financial-services sector. It could be expected that other states will soon follow with similar state-mandated cybersecurity requirements.

While the fairness of these complex mandates can be debated, one cannot argue that hackers are aggressively targeting the financial-services sector. In 2016 hackers stole $81 million from Bangladesh Central Bank via its Society for Worldwide Interbank Financial Telecommunications (SWIFT) messaging service. They later repeated the crime using the same SWIFT messaging service on Ecuadorian bank Banco del Austro. Hackers exploited a vulnerability by sending what appeared to be authentic messages that were used to conduct unauthorized wire transfers. Investigators uncovered evidence that the Bangladesh Central Bank was using secondhand $10 network switches without a firewall to run its network. This gave hackers access to the bank's entire infrastructure, including the SWIFT servers. (Source: http://thehackernews.com/2016/04/bank-firewall-security.html.)

Approximately eleven thousand banks and other financial institutions use the SWIFT system to send and receive payment instructions through a standardized system of codes. These attacks put them all on high alert, and the Federal Financial Institutions Examination Council issued guidance to banks.

The Bangladesh heist is summarized in the graphic below:

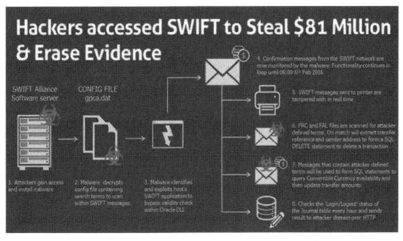

(Source: thehackernews.com/2016/04/swift-bank-hack.html.)

Utilities

As far as public records show, the utility sector has not had nearly as many cyberattacks as other sectors, such as health care, retail, and financial services. However, the number of attacks, or attempted attacks, may be greater than we think. The nature of network-security incidents and the data that may have been compromised may determine what the affected organization is legally obligated to reveal publicly. For example, an attack on critical infrastructure may not affect personally identifiable information, and there may not be a legal obligation to notify anyone. However, a successful attack could be far-reaching and perhaps catastrophic for the public at large.

Consider a quote from the Department of Energy's 2016 report on the state of the cybersecurity of our power grids: "Widespread disruption of electric service because of a transmission failure initiated by a cyberattack at various points of entry could undermine US lifeline networks, critical defense infrastructure, and much of the economy; it could also endanger the health and safety of millions of citizens…Also, natural gas plays an increasingly important role as fuel for the nation's electricity system; a gas pipeline outage or malfunction due to a cyberattack could affect not only pipeline and related infrastructures, but also the reliability of the nation's electricity system." (Source: https://energy.gov/sites/prod/files/2017/01/f34/QER%20 Transforming%20the%20Nations%20Electricity%20 System%20Full%20Report.pdf.)

Ted Koppel wrote about these vulnerabilities in frightening detail in his best-selling book *Lights Out*. He describes how, since the time that our power industry was deregulated more than forty years ago, thousands of small, privately owned companies are transmitting power from the power source to the end user. It is doubtful that these companies have significant resources to fend off a sophisticated cyberattack. Their activities are coordinated by supervisory control and data acquisition (SCADA) systems. They can help balance supply and demand in different parts of the country, as power demand rises and falls in specific geographic regions. Koppel raised the question of SCADA itself being vulnerable to cyberattack, which could literally knock out power to vast areas. Compounding the cyberthreat to the power grids is the fact that their proper operation depends on large power transformers. The main concern is how difficult they are to replace if physically destroyed. Each one has a customized design, and they are mostly made overseas and are extremely difficult to transport, weighing four hundred thousand to six hundred thousand pounds. It is estimated that it would take more than a year to replace one. Consider a cyberattack on SCADA and the independent companies transmitting power in conjunction with a physical attack on the transformers, and it is feasible that a significant power outage could, in fact, happen.

Koppel not only described how the power grids are susceptible to cyberattack but also revealed just how unprepared both individuals and our government are to deal with a lengthy power outage. If millions of people across a vast geography were without power for several weeks or months, chaos would ensue. No heating or refrigeration, no sewage, no food or medical care over a several-month period could lead not only to economic collapse but the death of all but a small minority of people affected by the outage.

Koppel is careful not to create the impression that an attack on our power grids is easy or even likely to happen, but his research seems to provide proof that it is entirely possible. After *Lights Out* was published, we saw a cyberattack actually take out Ukraine's power grid. Investigators determined that the outage was, in fact, caused by a cyberattack and concluded that malware known as Black Energy was used to carry out the successful attack. Power went out for only half a day, but it seems to prove that Koppel is on to something and that we can expect power-grid attacks to happen in the future.

We could devote several pages of this book to how to prepare for such a cataclysmic event. However, the reality is that most organizations would not follow anything close to that plan. The few that did would have their best laid disaster plans trampled on by a crazed and desperate majority that did not and would surely lose the fight for whatever precious resources remain.

CHAPTER 5

Preventing an Attack: Defense Strategies

Now that business leaders have a general understanding of the network-security and privacy-liability risks associated with being online, they must start strategizing how, if at all, they can prevent becoming the next hacking victim. Traditionally, just getting to this point has been a struggle. All too often, we have seen a tug-of-war play out among employees with competing interests. The IT security team may realize a potential risk, but it must convince the C-suite to put in the necessary time and effort to understand the risk and deploy the essential resources for preventive controls. It is not a fun conversation but a necessary one in our risk-filled digital age.

Prevention strategies will differ from organization to organization. Budgets, corporate culture, leadership, industry vertical, and geography will all influence how serious an effort will be made in preventing an attack. Once a decision is made to organize and implement defenses, the effort will focus on three areas: technology, people, and processes. But before pouring resources into cyberattack defense, business leaders first need a good history lesson. As the saying goes, you don't know where you are going until you know where you have been. Understanding the different attacks that hackers historically have carried out will help determine which tools are needed to fight a particular battle. Determine the most common ways hackers are coming after businesses, update your technology, educate your workforce, and adapt your processes.

To that end, we will be focusing on three of the most common types of network-intrusion attacks: social-engineering attacks, distributed denial-of-service attacks, and ransomware attacks. Each attack requires somewhat differing techniques. The weapons you choose will have a significant impact on chances of preventing or, at the very least, mitigating the effects of a successful attack.

Social Engineering

Given the rising incidence of social-engineering fraud, all companies should implement basic risk-avoidance measures:

- Your employees can be your weakest link or your greatest asset as your first defense in the fight against cybercrime. A formal education process should be created so that employees can learn to be vigilant and recognize fraudulent behavior. E-mail is likely the way the perpetrator will carry out a social-engineering attack, so focus efforts on that attack vector first. Employees need to know that they should not open spam or unsolicited e-mail from unknown parties and especially that they should never click on links in the e-mail. These often contain malware that will give criminals access to your computer system.

Training can be done in various ways:

- **Break room approach**: Organize in-person meetings for all employees on what to do when they receive e-mails from unknown sources.
- **Periodic security videos**: When in-person meetings are not possible, have employees view short security-awareness training videos and webinars.
- **Phishing-test approach**: Test all or preselect certain employees, and send them a simulated phishing attack. Your goal will be get employees to recognize a dangerous e-mail and report it to the appropriate IT security authority immediately. There will undoubtedly be those who do exactly that, but unfortunately, there will be a certain employee population who clicks on the malicious attachment or link. Those who fail the phishing test should be immediately made aware of their misstep and perhaps view a pop-up training video at the moment they click on the attachment or e-mail.

Your training program does not necessarily have to be punitive. Instead, consider an approach of rewarding your cyber defense all-stars and identifying those who need a better education. It should involve interactive elements and be continuous in nature, with regular follow-ups. It should simulate real-life attacks, and the training program's effectiveness should be monitored.

- Avoid free web-based e-mail, which tends to be less secure; instead, establish a private company domain, and use it to create valid e-mail accounts.
- Do not use the "reply" option to respond to any financial e-mails. Instead, use the "forward" option, and use the correct e-mail address, or select it from the e-mail address book to ensure the intended recipient's correct e-mail address is used.
- Beware of sudden changes in business practices. For example, if a current business contact suddenly asks to be contacted via his or her personal e-mail address when all previous official correspondence has been on a company e-mail, the request could be fraudulent.
- Establish a procedure requiring any verbal or e-mailed request for funds or information transfer to be confirmed in person or via phone by the individual supposedly making the request.
- Consider two-factor authorization for high-level IT and financial-security functions and dual signatures on wire transfers greater than a certain monetary threshold.

- Be careful of what is posted to social media and company websites, especially job duties/descriptions, hierarchal information, and out-of-office details. The more you publicize, the easier it is for someone to impersonate someone from your organization.

Despite these efforts, organizations can still fall victim to a social-engineering scheme. These incidents can be reported to the joint FBI/National White Collar Crime Center—Internet Crime Complaint Center (IC3) at www.ic3.gov.

Distributed Denial-of-Service Attacks

There are several strategies an organization can deploy to prevent a DDoS attack or at least mitigate the effects of one:

- Set traffic thresholds. Companies can track how many users typically visit their website during any given day, hour, and minute. Volume can change based on a number of factors. By having this historical knowledge, thresholds can be installed, and real-time alerts can be generated to advise of abnormal traffic.
- Blacklist and whitelist. Control who can and cannot access your network with whitelists and blacklists for specific IP addresses. However, be mindful that certain IP addresses may generate false positives and be blacklisted when they are, in fact, legitimate

traffic. By temporarily blocking traffic, a business can see how it responds. Legitimate users usually try again after a few minutes. Illegitimate traffic tends to switch IP addresses. A good resource to help begin the process of whitelisting and blacklisting can be found on the DNS whitelist at https://www.dnswl.org/. Here, you will find IP addresses, domain names, and e-mail contact addresses. Each IP address is given a trustworthiness level score.

- Reroute traffic with additional servers. By having additional servers on standby to handle an abnormal increase in traffic, a business can improve its odds against one server being overwhelmed. While this is likely the most cost-effective method, it is difficult to tell how many might be needed, since the size of the attack can vary.
- Consider using content-delivery networks (CDN). This method involves using external resources to identify illegitimate traffic and diverting it to a cloud-based infrastructure.
- There may be contractual obligations that are affected during and after a DDoS attack. Consequently, it is important to review contractual liability implications with customers and business partners. Review contracts with an eye toward the following:
  - Revise unfavorable service-guarantee language concerning downtime resulting from a DDoS attack. Allocate liability for potential outages as appropriate.

- Clauses that require security-incident notification under contract may be detrimental, especially when not required by law. Be sure your attorney reviews language related to this specific issue.
- Terminate traffic as soon as a DDoS attack starts. Terminate unwanted connections or processes on servers and routers and tune their TCP/IP settings. If the bottleneck is a particular a feature of an application, temporarily disable that feature.
- Analyze traffic and adjust defenses. If possible, use a network-analyzer tool to review the traffic. Create a network-intrusion-detection system signature to differentiate between benign and malicious traffic. If adjusting defenses, make one change at a time, so you know the cause of the changes you may observe. Configure egress filters to block the traffic your systems may send in response to DDoS traffic, to avoid adding unnecessary packets to the network.
- Notify and activate your incident-response team, if one is already in place. Contact the company's executive and legal teams. Upon their direction, consider involving law enforcement, and collaborate with your business-continuity/disaster-recovery team.
- Understand business implications. DDoS attacks may lead to significant business-interruption costs, lost income, reputational harm, and other

expenses. There may be a need to access funding or engage insurance companies, if applicable.

- Create a communication plan. A company can easily become overwhelmed with inquiries from customers, business partners, and media during a DDoS attack. Create a status page with a statement explaining the circumstances of the event. In addition, a template letter can be created to automatically respond to customers who contact a business for information.

- Document the incident. During a DDoS attack, immediate efforts should be made to document facts in an incident report. It should be used to document what happened, why it happened, decisions made, and how the organization will prevent future attacks. Review and document the load and logs of servers, routers, firewalls, applications, and other affected infrastructure. The incident report may be read by a wide audience, and it is therefore important that it not be written in overly technical language.

Ransomware

During the past year, we have seen ransomware attacks become more sophisticated with levels encryption that are very difficult, if not impossible, to break. The ransomware epidemic has evolved into a formal business model among hacking groups. While some attack campaigns are time consuming and require significant technical expertise, some hackers are willing to expend the required resources, for the payoff can be immense. These attacks can infect thousands of computers, causing massive operational disruption. Some attacks include backup systems, leaving the victims with little choice but to pay the ransom demands of the hacker.

It is therefore more important than ever to take steps to avoid being caught in a hacker's ransomware web. The FBI has weighed in on this matter and offered advice on their website:

- The most effective defense against ransomware is to back up data files. Data stored on a corporate user's network drive is usually backed up at regular intervals. However, it is not standard practice to back up a user's desktop. Consider keeping multiple copies of data.
- Employee training is important. Most ransomware attacks are carried out through phishing e-mails targeted at employees. Training should focus on the latest trends and should take place on an ongoing basis.
- Disable macro scripts from office files transmitted via e-mail. Consider using a propriety spam-scoring algorithm to monitor all incoming e-mail traffic, and filter out e-mails with potentially unsafe attachments and links.

- Implement software-restriction policies or other controls to prevent the execution of programs in common ransomware locations, such as temporary folders supporting popular Internet browsers and compression/decompression programs, including those located in the AppData/LocalAppData folder.
- Make sure antivirus and antimalware solutions are configured to automatically update and to conduct regular scans. Some other considerations can be highly dependent on organizational budget and system configuration.
- Implement application whitelisting. Only allow systems to execute programs known and permitted by security policy.
- Use virtualized environments to execute operating-system environments or specific programs.
- Categorize data based on organizational value, and implement physical/logical separation of networks and data for different organization units. For example, sensitive research or business data should not reside on the same server and/or network segment as an organization's e-mail environment.
- Restrict permissions by only allowing access to data on a need-to-know basis. The best way to save data and restrict access is to write backup to a DropFolder and only allow full control to a specific high-security user. To create a DropFolder, grant the Write permission to everyone, and grant the Read/List/Delete permission to the manager who

can recover files from the folder. (Source: *Enterprise Survival Guide for Ransomware Attacks*, by Shafqat Mehmood.)

- Change settings and enable blocking features to prevent the execution of malware at the initial stage. This should be done carefully and gradually, starting with a group of less critical users. (Source: *Enterprise Survival Guide for Ransomware Attacks*, by Shafqat Mehmood.)
- Require user interaction for end-user applications communicating with websites uncategorized by the network proxy or firewall. Examples include requiring users to type information or enter a password when their system communicates with a website uncategorized by the proxy or firewall.

(Source: https://www.fbi.gov/news/stories/incidents-of-ransomware-on-the-rise.)

Should an organization fall victim to ransomware, there may be a way to decrypt the data via various tools found for free on the Internet. Fightransomware.com is one website that lists the latest decryption tools available:

Bring Your Own Device (BYOD)

Employee use of mobile devices to transact business has become the norm for most modern-day companies. For many, it is a necessity. The struggle between efficient business practices and device security has driven many to formulate formal BYOD policies to create a balance between these two often-competing priorities.

There is a running joke in the cybersecurity industry. The BYOD acronym does not stand for "bring your own device." No, it actually stands for "bring your own disaster." This kind of dark humor, while getting chuckles in the industry, is well founded. A 2016 survey of 882 cybersecurity professionals, representing ten countries, who are part of the Information Security Community on LinkedIn, revealed some troubling findings:

- One in five organizations suffered a mobile-security breach, primarily driven by malware and malicious Wi-Fi.
- Only 34 percent of companies wipe sensitive data from employees' devices when they leave the company.
- Security threats to BYOD impose heavy burdens on organizations' IT resources (35 percent) and help-desk workloads (27 percent).

(Source: http://www2.blancco.com/en/research-study/2016-byod-and-mobile-security-studyof.)

Despite the reality of online threats to mobile-device use, they will continue to be used in the workplace for the foreseeable future. Organizations need to take steps to formulate, implement, and enforce a formal BYOD program. Here are some policies to consider:

The Device

Consider the types of devices that will be supported, bearing in mind that a consistent user experience will be expected. Decide whether it will be a "corporate-owned, personally enabled" (COPE) or a "corporate-owned, business-only" (COBO) strategy. Address password requirements, device disposal, employee terminations, and procedures to follow after a device is lost. Consider software for monitoring and wiping the device when needed.

Device Usage

Decide whether or not to limit participation in the BYOD program to certain employees, based on job functions. In addition, consider whether or not certain restrictions should be placed on the types of work product data that can be accessed from mobile devices. Require periodic employee acknowledgments of the BYOD policy.

Organizations need to anticipate data-privacy issues when employees will be traveling abroad. Multiple jurisdictional privacy laws should be anticipated. Certain countries may have strict data-control measures. Others may create hostile environments where border control agents may look to search devices.

Implementing and Enforcing the BYOD Policy

The best way to mitigate legal liability and promote compliance is to have a clear, top-down approach applicable to all employees. It should contain realistic compliance requirements and should be consistently enforced. However, this should be measured against the benefits—including often-increased productivity—that may come with a more flexible approach. An individual should be assigned to stay abreast of evolving privacy laws that may impact the BYOD policy. Significant updates need to be communicated to the workforce.

Tips for Securing Mobile Devices

BYOD policies may also contain tips for employees to help secure their mobile devices. Consider these security tips:

- Connecting to secure, password-protected wireless networks can be dangerous, but connecting to unsecured networks is reckless. Configure mobile devices to refuse connections to unsecured wireless networks.
- Be wary of any permission requested by mobile applications.
- Disable unnecessary permissions for applications.
- Bluetooth should be either off or hidden from discovery.
- Block the use of third-party software where possible.
- Enable password protections or biometric security on devices.
- Turn on encryption.
- Implement remote wipe capabilities on the device.

- Delete "stale" or "dead" apps that are no longer being maintained by the developer, since any needed security updates will probably not take place within these apps.
- Update mobile devices frequently when they become available, since the vast majority of updates are security patches.
- Do not "jailbreak" or "root" phones. Jailbreaking is the process of removing software restrictions, while "rooting" modifies the operating systems. Both allow for user privilege escalation.
- Download mobile-security applications as they become available.
- Do not put your phone number on social media sites or give it to unknown parties. Some social media sites, such as dating applications, are inherently dangerous.

Password Management

For several years organizations required their employees to use passwords as one of the means to secure data. Passwords are probably the most prevalent end-user data-protection method. Password management has improved over time, as awareness of password-management best practices has gone mainstream. It is a best practice not to use easily guessable passwords and to change them often. Unfortunately, as evidenced by a recent report by security firm Keeper Security, many people are not following this advice. The firm recently compiled a list of ten million passwords that were exposed publicly in recent data breaches. Of the ten million passwords analyzed, "123456" was the most popular password, used nearly 17 percent of the time.

Hackers commonly use brute-force attacks to crack passwords that may not be found in a dictionary. They often use devices that cost less than a thousand dollars and are capable of testing billions of passwords per second. They might try combinations of known passwords such as commonly used terms in pop culture, as well as names, phone numbers, or birthdays.

Below is a list that Keeper Security published in January 2017.

The Top Twenty-Five Most Common Passwords of 2016

1. 123456
2. 123456789
3. qwerty
4. 12345678
5. 111111
6. 1234567890
7. 1234567
8. password
9. 123123
10. 987654321

11. qwertyuiop
12. mynoob
13. 123321
14. 666666
15. 18atcskd2w
16. 7777777
17. 1q2w3e4r
18. 654321
19. 555555
20. 3rjs1la7qe
21. google
22. 1q2w3e4r5t
23. 123qwe
24. zxcvbnm
25. 1q2w3e

(Source: https://blog.keepersecurity.com/2017/01/13/most-common-passwords-of-2016-research-study/.)

To avoid these mistakes, a formal password-management program should be emphasized. In a recent article published by *Wired* magazine, experts weighed in and recommended the following points to consider:

- Password length is more important than password complexity.
- Avoid common terms in sports and pop culture.
- Use digits, symbols, and capital letters. Make sure you spread them throughout the middle of your password, not at the beginning or end.

- Don't use the same password on multiple websites. If one is compromised, hackers may try your password on other popular websites.
- Avoid requiring password changes too often. This could cause users to make small changes that won't necessarily make them more secure.
- Passwords should be considered only one part of a layered approach. Consider using passwords with other means to identify an individual, such as biometric data.

(Source: https://www.wired.com/2016/05/password-tips-experts/.)

Vendor Management

Even after securing networks, training employees, and shifting to more secure processes, a good cyber-risk manager will realize that the work is not yet done. Many times, it is necessary to use outside vendors that will have access to an organization's most sensitive data. On a daily basis, vendors are entrusted with their clients' sensitive data and are given direct access to their networks via billing systems and other Internet-connected channels. There is good reason for a cyber-risk manager to be concerned. According to the 2016 Ponemon study, approximately one in four data breaches is caused by a third party. In fact, many of these were headline news:

- **Target, November 2013**: Hackers stole network-access credentials from an outsourced HVAC contractor to gain access to Target's systems, compromising forty million payment cards of Target customers. (http://krebsonsecurity.com/2014/02/target-hackers-broke-in-via-hvac-company/.)
- **Office of Personnel Management, June 2015:** Hackers gained access to a contractor's credentials to access security-clearance data of more than twenty-one million government employees, including fingerprints, social security numbers, addresses, employment history, and financial records.
(https://www.securelink.com/securelink-blog/opm-guide-vendor-breaches/.)
- **T-Mobile, September 2015**: Hackers accessed the network of an outsourced background-check company to access the names, birth dates, addresses, and social security and driver's license numbers of fifteen million T-Mobile customers.

Many privacy statutes require that the organization that originally collected the sensitive information conduct or oversee a proper investigation and notify the affected individuals and regulators. So the organization can't easily escape liability or costs, even though their vendor may have been at fault for failing to secure the data. This cyber-risk management issue has given rise to the concept of vendor-management programs with an eye toward managing a vendor's cyber risk. Since most vendor relationships are carried out through written contracts, they need to be modified to address this critical issue.

Vendor management should be a central part of a cyber-risk management agenda, regardless of industry sector. Some common vendors by industry include the following:

- Health care: medical billing firms and labs
- Retail: payment processors
- Higher education: loan application processors
- Municipalities: outsourced IT, background-check firms, and payroll processors
- Information technology: subcontracted IT and cloud providers
- Financial services: mortgage applications and ATM services
- Legal: expert witnesses, stenographers, and copy shops

There are industry-specific privacy regulations and proposed legislation in business sectors that require particular attention when managing vendor risk:

Health care: HIPAA rules require covered entities to enter into formal agreements with their business associates. This requirement applies to vendors that act on behalf of or provide services to a covered entity that involves access to protected health information.

Retail: PCI DSS 3.0 and 3.1 emphasize the merchants' responsibility to address vulnerabilities from third-party vendors, partners, and service providers with access to cardholder data. PCI compliance requires merchants to "maintain a written agreement that includes an acknowledgment that the service providers are responsible for the security of cardholder data the service providers possess or otherwise store, process, or transmit on behalf of the customer, or to the extent that they could impact the security of the customer's cardholder data environment." (Source: http://www.dataprotectionreport.com/2015/05/pci-dss-3-0-requires-some-service-provider-contract-changes/.)

In addition, they are required to keep records of vendor-penetration tests, vulnerability scans, and assessments as part of vendor-risk management.

Financial services: The New York Department of Financial Services cybersecurity regulations require financial-service companies to have formal policies and procedures for third-party service-provider management. Their vendors must utilize encryption and multifactor authentication, provide notice of incidents, and allow financial-service companies to perform network-security audits on vendor systems. Vendors are also required to indemnify and provide network-security warranties to financial-service clients.

Higher education: Pending legislation aims to amend the Family Education Rights and Privacy Act (FERPA).

The amendment would require colleges and universities to maintain and make available a list of all outside companies that have access to their students' information; give parents the right to review and correct personal information collected about their children by educational apps, online homework software, or any other school vendors; and minimize the amount of students' personal information that schools could transfer to other companies.

Information technology: EU safe harbor rules that once allowed the transfer of EU residents' data beyond EU borders were recently invalidated. Organizations continue to rely on outsourced cloud providers to manage their data; these providers often transfer the data to servers around the world. They should be mindful that wrongful data transfer in the eyes of an EU regulator can lead to significant fines. Regulations are proposed to allow for fines up to 4 percent of a company's annual revenue.

Here are the key areas to focus on in creating a comprehensive vendor-management program:

Contracts: Vendor contracts need to address roles and responsibilities in the event of a data breach. Contract terms should be specific as to incident response and liability for costs. Contracts should address who leads the incident investigation, which incident-response vendors will be hired, and which party will control communications.

Cloud providers: Cloud-provider contracts, especially those with the larger cloud providers, pose particular challenges. There is an inherent aggregation risk, as many cloud providers maintain the data of thousands of clients. As a result, they rarely allow for favorable indemnification provisions and will mandate their own definitions of "reasonable security standards." Should a breach occur in the cloud network, the cloud provider may be dealing with thousands of affected clients. The affected cloud-provider clients will most certainly run into issues such as control of the response, access to data, investigation, preservation of evidence, and e-discovery, regardless of contract terms.

Cloud providers may also disperse data across multiple servers and different geographic locations. This can conflict with international laws restricting cross-border data transfer. At minimum, companies utilizing cloud providers should understand where their data subjects reside, require prior notification if data is to be transferred to other servers, and maintain a compliance plan for all cross-border transfers.

Vendor cybersecurity warranties: Vendors should be required to maintain minimum network-security standards. Compliance should be validated at least once each year via an independent network assessment. The assessment should audit technology and expand to an evaluation of potential vulnerabilities posed by vendor employees and procedures. Vendors should be required to share the audit results.

Insurance: In the event a vendor's negligence causes a breach of its clients' sensitive data, the clients most certainly will incur costs. Crisis-management costs for defense counsel, IT forensics, notification, credit monitoring, and public-relations fees can easily reach six figures and beyond. Insurance is a means of shifting costs to or recovering costs from the vendor. Unfortunately, organizations often rely solely on a vendor's certificate of insurance, with limited information about the coverage. Certificates typically state that the vendor has a current insurance policy and a specific limit of coverage. The current cyber insurance market is crowded with dozens of insurance companies writing the policies, all with unique terms, conditions, and exclusions. A certificate of insurance indicating $1 million in insurance coverage may fail to indicate that the policy contains a crisis-management sublimit of one hundred thousand dollars, which could greatly restrict recovery. Certificates may not clarify whether or not the policy contains exclusions for lack of encryption or acts of foreign governments, contractual exclusions, restrictions on geographic territory, and "other insurance" provisions making vendor insurance secondary to that of their clients. Therefore, a thorough review of the vendor's insurance policy is needed.

Claims and litigation management: Should litigation arise as a result of a data breach of a company's data while in the hands of a vendor, a question may arise as to where the case will be adjudicated. Choice of law can have a significant impact on the outcome in court. Legal concepts and their interpretations may be broadly construed in one state or country and narrowly applied in another. As US firms continue to outsource functions around the globe, consideration should be given to the optimal geographic location for dispute resolution, which should be clearly outlined in the vendor contract.

Businesses have come to the unfortunate conclusion that, as long as they remain connected to a network, they and their vendors remain vulnerable to attacks. Their data is their lifeblood, and businesses have taken extraordinary steps to protect it. There is a clear and growing need to manage their risk after data leaves the confines of their castle and is handed to vendors.

Understand that some organizations will have greater leverage than others when sitting down to negotiate contract terms related to cyber risk. Making demands of a multinational vendor with thousands of clients will most likely be a waste of time and energy. These vendors will not have the incentive or the wherewithal to negotiate individual contracts with all their clients. Instead, focus your time and energy on the smaller vendors, who will be more willing to negotiate. The focus should be on everything we have been asking each organization to include:

- Require cybersecurity audits at least annually. Ask the vendor to share the results of each audit.
- Require employee background checks.

- Address roles and responsibilities of both the organization and the vendor in a breach response. Ideally, the organization that originally collected the data should seek to control the investigation and the communication process.
- Both the organization and the vendor will most certainly incur costs in a data-breach response. Demand that the vendor provide proof of insurance as a means of cost recovery. Require favorable indemnification language in the contract.
- Have a contingency plan to use alternate vendors, since a cyberattack on a vendor may make it inoperable for some time, and thus it will unable to perform critical functions for the organization.

International Cybersecurity Standards

There are several cybersecurity standards that any organization can look to for additional guidance. Many of these were produced by academia and leading members of the public and private sectors. Compliance with these standards often satisfies the authorities that regulate privacy security matters. Some common standards include the following:

- **National Institute of Standards and Technology's cybersecurity framework**: A framework that provides a structure for organizations to create, assess, or improve their cybersecurity programs (https://www.nist.gov/)

- **ISO 27000 standards**: An international standard that provides a set of information-security controls (http://www.27000.org/index.htm)
- **Common criteria for information technology security (ISO/IEC 15408)**: International standards and guidelines used for evaluating information-security products via quality-assurance processes
- **COBIT**: A framework for developing, implementing, monitoring, and improving IT governance and management practices (http://www.isaca.org/knowledge-center/cobit/pages/overview.aspx)
- **Cloud security alliance cloud computing matrix**: A baseline set of security controls to help organizations assess risk associated with cloud providers (https://cloudsecurityalliance.org/group/cloud-controls-matrix/)
- **Payment card industry data-security standard**: A group founded in 2006 by representatives from American Express, Discover, JCB International, MasterCard, and Visa Inc., it sets the data-security standards for entities that process, store, or transmit payment cardholder data. (https://www.pcisecuritystandards.org/pci_security/)

Understand that not every one of these resources will be appropriate for all organizations. The controls imposed by some of their standards may not be realistic for smaller, less complex organizations.

CHAPTER 6

Responding to an Attack: Saving Your Bottom Line and Your Reputation

Enterprise risk managers are tasked with anticipating every conceivable risk posed to their respective companies. There is no shortage of risks. They can include natural hazards, shareholder lawsuits, product liability, product recall, political risk, civil unrest, and regulatory risk. The list goes on and on. These managers will often take a methodical approach to each risk by taking steps to change the probability of the threat coming to bear or preparing in advance to mitigate the damage if it occurs. They may look to share the risk with others or fully retain the risk by making informed decisions. This is a critical role and one that may report directly to senior officials, including the CEO.

Unfortunately for enterprise risk managers, they have a new risk in the form of cyber risk that will surely keep them awake at night. The stark reality is simple: if you rely on a network, you are faced with some amount of cyber risk. Regulatory authorities, attorneys general, business partners, shareholders, and clients all expect that efforts are made to truly understand the risk and that resources are devoted to managing it. Fortunately, many risk professionals have taken the threat seriously. In a 2015 study by Advisen, 92 percent believe cyber risks pose at least a moderate threat to their organizations. In the same study, 68 percent of board members stated that cyber risks pose a significant threat to their respective organizations. As a result, many leaders are starting to focus on ways to manage the cyber threats.

One way to do this is to create a formal incident-response plan. While cyberdefense tools may be in place, there is no 100 percent guarantee that they will prevent a cyberattack. Therefore, a game plan to react to an attack is critical and sometimes contractually or statutorily required. Many organizations have some form of a plan in place. Advisen's 2015 survey revealed that 72 percent have a plan in place focused on reducing the potential crisis-management costs, reputational damages, and business-interruption losses. The plans will differ from one organization to another. Factors driving these differences include the organization's size and structure, industry regulations, and client requirements. They can be one page to fifty pages long. However, there are several components that are included in most plans to facilitate cyber resilience in the aftermath of an attack.

To begin the planning process, it is critical to understand what data the organization collects, stores, and processes. This may include sensitive corporate material, trade secrets, personally identifiable information, personal health information, and payment-card and banking information. If any of that data is compromised, the plan should be designed to mitigate financial and reputational harm while meeting obligations imposed by law, business partners, clients, and anyone else. It should outline procedures to counter losses that result from a wide range of sources, including third-parties, contractors, employees, or state-actors of foreign governments.

The plan should consider simulated situations that include corrupted, lost, or stolen data; hackers gaining access to data through a malicious attack; and employee negligence. There should be assumptions that data could be affected by a variety of scenarios and targeted attacks. These may include distributed denial-of-service attacks, ransomware infections, and social-engineering schemes.

Here is a breakdown of key components that should be included in every network-security incident-response plan:

The Incident Report Form

It is extremely important to capture the initial information of an incident as quickly as possible. A clear reporting form and format will provide that foundation. This initial information might be needed for investigative purposes in both the near and distant future. Understand that it will be read by a wide range of people, both inside and outside the organization. It may be deemed discoverable evidence in future litigation. The CEO, business partners, clients, plaintiff attorneys, regulators, insurance companies, and media outlets could conceivably have access to it. Therefore, it should be as accurate as possible. This can prove to be a difficult process in the early stages of an incident. There will likely be more questions than answers at this point, but a documented, good-faith effort to understand what happened is needed regardless.

To provide this, the incident form should capture any system event logs, a description of the event, what actions have been taken, decisions made or not made, and a mechanism to classify the type of event that occurred. Common classifications of events may include data types, such as paper records, electronic records, intellectual property, or financial records. It should also classify sources of the cause, such as unauthorized or accidental disclosure, improper communications, wrongful disposal, theft, or extortion. The incident report should contain an initial assessment of the nature, scope, and root cause of the incident. The early assessment will determine next steps, such as the type of assistance needed and anticipated remedial efforts. Estimates of the gravity of the situation can be classified. "Low severity" may involve little or no private data. "Moderate severity" may include some private data implicated with damage limited to the internal parts of the organization. Finally, a

"Severe" classification would involve a significant amount of private data or a network disruption that will likely lead to a material negative financial impact.

The Internal Incident Response Team

Network intrusions usually require a response involving a cross section of individuals within an organization. It therefore makes sense to build an incident-response team before an event occurs. It would not be uncommon to have at least one individual representing legal, communications, compliance, risk management, information technology, operations, finance, human resources, and sales. The team may assign an overall crisis manager who would report to executive management. Smaller, less sophisticated companies will often have one person representing more than one department.

Once the team is in place, specific roles and responsibilities should be assigned to each individual. Once an incident is identified, individuals should be assigned specific responsibilities and empowered to make decisions. Who will escalate an issue, and how will they do this? How far up the ladder should it be communicated? Who will manage and document the investigation? How will evidence be preserved? Who will communicate with law enforcement, insurance companies, employees, business partners, and the press? It is conceivable that disputes, stress, and confusion could overwhelm a staff in a time-sensitive scenario involving critical-data compromise. A spokesperson will naturally want to communicate the facts, while general counsel may be hardwired not to say anything unless he or she legally has to. Meanwhile, IT staff is trying to figure out what happened and may need additional resources to investigate and preserve the evidence. They may need to disable critical network systems to do this. Would this create even further chaos? Human resources may feel the need to do something for employees if their own data was compromised, but what?

All this will certainly lead to unforeseen costs, so the finance and accounting departments should be called in to immediately allocate funds. These can easily approach six figures. Meanwhile, if sensitive personally identifiable information has been compromised, the clock is ticking, since regulators might require notice of the event within just a few weeks. Failure to meet these deadlines can lead to significant fines and bad press and fuel the fire of plaintiff attorneys, who might sue the organization on behalf of the affected individuals. As all this is sorted out, it may become apparent that the attack is still happening and could affect the incident-response team members' own mobile devices, limiting their ability to perform. They may need to separate themselves from the attack vector. This may mean using new devices and off-band communications.

One can see how even the best-managed companies could mishandle a data-breach response if they have never been through one before and have never created a plan to map out critical roles and responsibilities. This can be the difference between a bad day and a catastrophic day for the affected organization.

Retaining External Vendors

Once the incident-response team is in place, it is important to note that many incidents will require expertise that likely does not exist within the organization. Complicated investigations and communication with the outside world are frequently mishandled and pose significant risk to any organization. Most communications structures include holding statements, incident notifications, internal and external FAQs, call-center preparedness, press releases, individual victim notifications, and state and federal regulator notifications. Each of these may need to be released at a different time during the response.

Outside vendors may include the following:

Privacy attorneys: An attorney who specializes in privacy law will be needed to determine what legal obligations the affected organization may have. The attorney will need to demonstrate expertise in privacy laws at the state, federal, and international level, since complying with these statutes may be required. It may be prudent to use the privacy attorney to hire any additional vendors needed to preserve attorney-client privilege should litigation arise at a future date. The privacy attorney will be one of the most important vendors in a data-breach response, since he or she will not only coordinate other vendors but may also be dealing with regulators and law enforcement. Costs can vary, depending on the level of experience—$350 to $900 per hour can be expected.

IT forensic investigators: These investigators will be critical in finding out how a network intrusion occurred, when the attack started, exactly what data was compromised, and when the attack ended, as well as in containing the situation with initial remediation efforts and helping preserve evidence. Any affected systems should be secured against physical access and left running after an incident occurs. If possible, the affected systems should be disconnected from any wired or wireless networks to ensure that evidence does not get contaminated, either intentionally by the perpetrator or unintentionally by someone who normally is authorized to access the system. The IT forensic investigator may suggest making forensic images of the affected computers, which could serve to preserve a snapshot of the system at the time of the incident for later analysis and potentially for use as evidence at trial. Spoliation and failure to preserve evidence can lead to increased litigation costs and adverse civil court decisions down the road, so make sure this is a priority. It is also important to understand that even the most experienced and capable IT forensic investigators may take several weeks to complete an investigation, since many attacks are sophisticated and can affect multiple servers or even an entire network. In addition to relevant experience, some important factors to consider are whether or not they have capacity to be deployed quickly and the cost, which can range from $350 to $550 per hour.

Mailing and call centers: An investigation may reveal that an organization is legally required to notify the affected individuals. In general, these letters notify people how the incident occurred, what information was compromised, what is being done to help victims, what the organization is doing to make sure it never happens again, and a phone number to call for additional information. Some incidents can involve several thousand and perhaps millions of individuals. These larger incidents may necessitate outsourcing the notification function, which includes printing letters, mailing letters, and managing return mail. It can be a monumental and time-consuming task. Outsourcing it can be the difference between meeting legal compliance for timely notice, as mandated by regulators, or missing it. In addition, the notification company may offer call-center services, since a certain population will call the number provided in the notification letter. Most organizations will not have the wherewithal to handle a significant number of calls.

One consideration would be to engage a call center to answer common questions. It would be a good idea to arm the call-center operator with answers to frequently asked questions. Give the operators a means to transfer calls to a designated individual within the organization if a caller seeks additional information. Take advantage of call-center technologies that allow access to real-time dashboards that may allow you to track caller wait times. Should call volume spike, wait times could grow, and this technology will allow you to deploy additional operators as needed.

Credit Monitoring and ID Theft Restoration

When notifying an affected population whose personally identifiable information may have been compromised, there may be an expectation that appropriate credit monitoring is provided. In fact, two US states require that it be offered under certain circumstances. Most organizations offer one year involving one, two, or three credit bureaus. However, others have offered two years. Certain attorneys general may request a specific number of years, and this should be taken into consideration.

Credit monitoring immediately notifies an individual if an attempt is made to obtain some form of credit in his or her name. In addition to monitoring, credit restoration services are usually offered in the event identity theft occurs. This is a valuable service that restores a victim's good credit, saves time, and alleviates stress. However, credit monitoring does not *prevent* identity theft. The only way to prevent an identity thief from accessing a victim's credit is to either place a ninety-day fraud alert on a credit file or freeze credit lines altogether.

- Fraud alerts require potential creditors to contact individuals before opening lines of credit. To activate a fraud alert, individuals are required to notify one of the three bureaus (Equifax, Experian, or TransUnion) and to repeat the process every ninety days to maintain the fraud-alert status.

- Freezing credit can be accomplished by contacting all three credit bureaus and requires each one to place a freeze on an individual's credit file. Each bureau provides a PIN that can be used to lift the freeze later. There may be a nominal fee based on state of residence, which typically ranges from five to fifteen dollars. Some states may allow an additional fee to lift the freeze. A credit freeze may cost less than credit monitoring and identity-theft restoration services, but it can cause other inconveniences for the individual. Credit checks cannot be performed while a freeze is in place. So those applying for a job, leasing a car, or renting an apartment will have to lift the credit freeze for this to occur.

Additional services may be offered as well, including dark-web searches to determine if specific identities are being actively sold on the black market. This is a more proactive measure and should be considered.

Public relations firms: When a data breach involves tens of thousands of individuals, there is a chance that local or national media may pick up on the news. This scenario often calls for issuing a holding statement early on, when all the facts are still unknown—a simple message with a contrite tone conveying only the facts needed. This will provide time for the investigation to unfold. Careful consideration should be given as to whether or not the organization can handle media inquiries. There may be a need to retain the services of a public-relations firm to handle these. Public-relations firms can play a significant part in communications that preserve the firm's reputation.

Law enforcement: It is prudent to notify law-enforcement authorities if criminal behavior is suspected. Start with local police. However, they may not have the resources to deal with certain cases, so consider also contacting your local FBI or US Secret Service. The increase in the number and scope of cyberattacks has led to significant attention from various law-enforcement agencies. This has led to more success in identifying and prosecuting the attackers. Law enforcement gathers significant intelligence on various groups responsible for these attacks. This may be beneficial to efforts to respond to, mitigate, and remediate attacks. Be aware that their investigation may be ongoing parallel to your own, and at times law-enforcement involvement may delay your own efforts to investigate the matter. Their involvement may also affect issues related to attorney-client privilege. Furthermore, law-enforcement agencies may be hesitant to share information. Organizations should therefore consult with legal counsel to evaluate the potential advantages and disadvantages of notifying law enforcement based on their specific circumstances.

Forensic accountants: There may be the need to tally the financial impact of a network-security incident for internal budgeting, insurance companies, and litigation. Lost clients, crisis-management expenses, legal fees, regulatory fines, class-action lawsuits, IT security remediation expenses, notification services, credit monitoring, and business-interruption costs can all come into play. Consider the services of a forensic accountant to help calculate both current and future financial losses.

For additional guidance, the Federal Trade Commission recently published its *Data Breach Response: A Guide for Business*, which is designed to help companies respond and mitigate costs in the aftermath of a network-security incident. The response guidelines organize post-breach actions into three categories: (1) secure operations, (2) fix vulnerabilities, and (3) notify appropriate parties. (Source: https://www.ftc.gov/system/files/documents/plain-language/pdf-0154_data-breach-response-guide-for-business.pdf.)

Further justification for taking the time and energy to create an incident-response team and a formal plan was evidenced in the 2016 IBM study. According to the study, using an incident-response team following a data breach was the single most important factor in reducing costs. Creating a team and following a plan led to an average cost saving of sixteen dollars per record. (Source: http://www.cnbc.com/2016/06/14/cost-of-data-breaches-hits-4-million-on-average-ibm.html.)

CHAPTER 7

Risk-Transfer Strategy: Cyber Insurance

As cyber threats evolved over the past twenty years, so have the means to transfer the risk. The commercial-insurance industry has always moved in lockstep with enterprise-wide threats, and its approach to cyber risk is no different. As the world came to realize that 100 percent reliance on IT security was not a realistic approach to fully managing the risk, a market for cyber insurance was born. As cyber threats became more common, the popularity of cyber insurance policies grew.

In the late 1990s, the industry began to address technology risk in the form of policies that covered financial losses due to errors and omissions from emerging technologies, which included the new frontiers of the Internet and e-commerce. However, these policies were limited in the coverage they provided. Coverage was limited to the failure of a computer system and did not include services needed to mitigate costs.

During the mid-2000s, the industry started to adapt to two distinct threats related to cyber risk. First, cybercriminals began to increase their attacks on networks that held payment-card data and other data that could be used for identity theft. Second, we started to see regulatory authorities begin to force businesses to comply with minimum security standards. These authorities began to flex their enforcement muscle in the form of fines against the offending entity. This drove the insurance industry to continue to evolve as policy forms adapted to meet the threats imposed by both hackers and regulators. Further contributing to growth was the fact that liabilities began to extend to executive leadership and board members. They have personally been the subject of lawsuits after recent data breaches. We started to see C-suite officers of these companies terminated as a direct result of a data breach. Fair or not, these executives were held accountable for not anticipating, preventing, or adequately responding to data breaches. Just a few years ago, executive leadership would never imagine such severe consequences for perceived lack of preparation for a cyberattack or inadequate response to one. Today, protracted litigation and firings are very real consequences and could be catastrophic for officers, boards, and directors.

Evidence of the growth of cyber insurance was recently highlighted in a report published by Allied Market Research, titled *Cyber Insurance Market—Global Opportunity Analysis and Industry Forecasts, 2014–2022,*" which states that the global cyber insurance market is expected to generate $14 billion in premiums by 2022. The largest cyber insurance market in 2015 was North America, with 87 percent of the market, and it is expected to keep dominating the market for the near future. Growth in this region was largely spurred by enforcement of US data-protection regulations. By contrast, there was a low penetration rate in developing countries that do not have robust privacy laws in place. The study also revealed that multiple industry sectors are buying cyber insurance, including health care, financial services, retail, information technology, utilities, energy, manufacturing, construction, and transportation. Of these sectors, health care dominates the market, with a one-third share. Large companies with annual revenues in excess of $1 billion purchase 70 percent of the cyber insurance policies.

Educating businesses and making them aware of their exposure to cyber risk is probably the biggest hurdle among insurance firms that want to provide cyber coverage to their markets. The NetDiligence 2015 study indicated that smaller firms, which tend not to purchase the coverage, are most likely to be attacked. It is an alarming trend, since the financial impact of a data breach may be too large for some of them to overcome. (Source: NetDiligence 2015 Cyber Claim Study.)

While they continue to evolve, many of today's cyber insurance policies usually cover the following exposures:

Network-security liability covers third-party damages resulting from a failure to protect against destruction, deletion, or corruption of a third party's electronic data. This could be the result of a denial-of-service attack against websites or computers or the transmission of a virus from third-party computers and systems.

Privacy liability covers third-party damages that result from the disclosure of confidential information collected or handled by you or that is under your custody or control. This includes coverage for vicarious liability if a vendor loses information you had entrusted to it.

Electronic-media content liability covers personal injury and trademark/copyright claims that arise from the creation and dissemination of electronic content.

Regulatory defense and penalties covers costs arising from an alleged violation of privacy law caused by a security breach.

Network extortion provides reimbursement for payments made under duress in response to an extortion threat.

Network business interruption provides reimbursement for your loss of income and extra expenses that result from an interruption or suspension of computer systems. This may include coverage for losses due to cyberattacks against other businesses that the organization relies on, known as dependent-business interruption coverage.

Data-breach event expenses covers costs associated with privacy regulation compliance. This includes retaining outside counsel, IT forensic investigators, credit monitoring, public-relations experts, mailing, and call centers.

Data asset protection covers costs and expenses that you may incur to restore, recreate, or recollect your data and other intangible assets.

One major challenge for the insurance buyer is that there is no such thing as a standard cyber insurance policy. Instead, each of the dozens of insurance companies that issue cyber insurance policies will write their own specific manuscript forms. Moreover, when the policy comes up for renewal, the policy terms are subject to change. There can be confusing language, exclusions, and limiting terms that might constrict or eliminate coverage altogether under certain circumstances. How one insurance carrier defines a "computer system" or a "failure of security" may differ from another, which can affect coverage. Some exclusions that might be found in a cyber insurance policy include losses resulting from

- loss of intellectual property or trade secrets;
- punitive damages that are not insurable under state law;
- loss of money or funds;
- costs to upgrade network systems to prevent future attacks;
- bodily injury and property damage;

- contractual liability;
- failure to encrypt data;
- acts of foreign governments;
- acts of war or "warlike actions," whether declared or not;
- violations of consumer-protection laws;
- failure to implement specific controls, such as "minimum required practices"; and
- losses caused by
  - mechanical failure;
  - error in design; or
  - gradual deterioration of computer systems.

This list is not all inclusive, so it is advisable to take the time to understand exactly where coverage pitfalls may exist. Insurance carriers will sometimes offer to cover these gaps by issuing policy endorsements.

Furthermore, it would be unwise to rely solely on traditional insurance policies to cover an organization for a cyber-risk-related event. Most of the underwriters of these policies have looked to completely, or at least partially, eliminate coverage. Here are just a few illustrations:

- Property insurance policies do not include malware and distributed denial-of-service attacks as "named perils," and they are usually not covered.
- General-liability insurance policies usually exclude coverage for losses due to cyberattacks.

- Crime-insurance policies generally cover only tangible property, not loss of data.
- Error-and-omissions insurance often requires negligence in professional services and usually does not cover costs related to regulatory actions.

Some additional points that the cyber insurance buyer should understand:

- Many of these policies require self-insured retentions, which can often range from $10,000 to $100,000 or even higher amounts. So the insured organization will be required to cover that amount before cyber insurance applies.
- There may also be sub-limits for certain categories of coverage. For example, a $1 million policy may limit cyber extortion payments to $50,000.
- There are also time limitations applied to network-interruption losses. Insurance companies will often impose waiting periods of eight to twelve hours before business interruption coverage will apply.
- Retroactive dates may apply, meaning incidents occurring before a certain date are excluded from coverage.
- Insurance companies may require using only their preapproved panel attorneys, IT forensics firms, and any other vendor that may assist in a network-security or privacy-liability event.
- Insurance companies often reserve the right to settle claims against at-fault parties and codefendants

in litigation, which can include an organization's key business partners and clients.

To be fair to the insurance companies, it should be noted that, as the markets evolve, they have begun to offer other valuable services meant to prevent a network intrusion or mitigate the effects of one. As one might expect, the higher the premium, the more preventive services the buyer generally gets. Some of these services may include

- cybersecurity risk assessments by cybersecurity firms;
- proactive dark web mining and monitoring of an insured's sensitive data to see if it is actively being sold;
- vendor security ratings to help an organization determine which vendors pose the greatest threat;
- services to identify known malicious IP addresses;
- insurance company mobile apps that provide real-time threat sharing and best practices; and
- online employee education and training.

One of the most fascinating developments in the cyber insurance market is the sheer number of insurance companies that dove head first into the cyber risk arena. As of this writing, there are more than seventy different insurance companies writing some form of cyber insurance, where just a few years ago there were only a handful. What makes this so surprising is the fact that the commercial insurance industry is traditionally a conservative one and one that takes great pains to understand risk before issuing a policy. But unlike traditional lines of insurance, such as property insurance, cyber insurers simply do not have a lot of actuarial data to make informed decisions. Property underwriters have studied decades worth of weather patterns, so they can predict with some degree of certainty where the next hurricane will hit. They know what kind of damages a level 4 hurricane may cause on Florida's west coast, because they know how many structures exist there and have a good idea of what it might cost to rebuild them. Their premiums are set to reflect this exposure. In contrast, the underwriting process in cyber insurance is much more difficult. If you were to ask someone what the probability of a cyberattack is, you might get a huge range of probabilities. Then, if you ask what an attack might cost, you will likely get a wide array of responses.

However, while the industry is in its infancy in terms of underwriting cyber risk, it is getting better as time goes by. Insurers have even started to partner with cybersecurity companies. Insurance and technology have created an unlikely partnership that continues to grow. Underwriters are now reaching out to cybersecurity firms to conduct penetration testing before writing a policy. They are learning to better understand risk profiles by asking many questions during the underwriting process. This process can be an application-heavy, time-consuming exercise, depending on the size and complexity of the organization that is applying for cyber insurance. Therefore, I have compiled a list of areas that an underwriter might focus on in the process. So before entering the market, do some soul searching and ask these questions about your organization's cyber hygiene:

- What industry am I in? Am I subject to strict regulations, such as HIPAA compliance or the minimum data-security standards that PCI imposes?
- What is my annual revenue?
- Do I have a formal data governance plan to address protective measures for data I collect, process, and store?
- When and how do I dispose of data?
- What security controls do I have in place? Have I benchmarked them against known standards, such as NIST, COBIT, and ISO?
- Am I operating in parts of the world that impose different data-security standards? What have I done to make sure I am in compliance?
- Do I have formal privacy policies, written information-security policies, business-continuity plans, and data-breach incident-response plans? How am I training my employees on these standards and putting these into practice?
- If vendors are either handling my sensitive data or have access to it, do I have a formal vendor-management program? Do my vendor contracts address cyber-risk exposure?
- How have I secured physical access to my workplace and to my paper files?

- Have I ever engaged a cybersecurity company to assess my vulnerabilities? If so, what were the positive and negative findings? How did I address any vulnerability that was identified in that process?

Although the cyber insurance–buying process can be cumbersome, there is some good news for the cyber insurance buyer. With so many cyber insurance carriers competing for business, there has been a large amount of capacity in the market. That competition has been one factor in keeping premiums relatively low. In addition, insurance carriers are increasing available limits.

Given the complexities of navigating the dynamic cyber insurance market, it is recommended that buyers engage the services of cyber insurance brokers and insurance consulting experts who are devoted to this sector of the insurance market. They often have key relationships with underwriters and in-depth knowledge of the latest products and services offered by cyber insurance companies and other vendors. They can also prepare organizations to be viewed in the most positive light possible when applying for cyber insurance. In addition, some offer additional services beyond securing cyber insurance. They can consult with an organization to make it cyber resilient by helping implement strategies to enhance the overall enterprise risk management program. Choosing the right brokerage or consulting firm and leveraging its products and services could translate to lower premiums and more favorable policy terms.

CHAPTER 8

High-Profile Attacks: What We Learned

I t seems that not a day goes by without news of another cyberattack. Hackers have kept up a relentless pace over the past several years. They have attacked individuals, government entities, nonprofit organizations, and businesses large and small. The hacks of just six companies—Yahoo, eBay, Anthem, Target, Chase, and Home Depot—combined for a compromise of *1.427 billion records*. The compromised records included payment cards, social security numbers, health records, and other detailed demographic information of individuals. To put that number into some perspective, consider that there are approximately 310 million residents of the United States. So the total number of compromised records related to these six attacks exceeds the US population several times over. It seems that nobody is immune.

In fact, a phrase I often hear repeated seems to ring true: there are three types of organizations, those that know they have been hacked, those that have been hacked and don't know it yet, and those that have been hacked again. Incredibly, those falling victim include those that have spent millions of dollars and devoted countless resources to the fight. It leads many to despair and wonder what else, if anything, can be done to turn the tide.

There is a silver lining. We can learn some valuable lessons by dissecting the events leading up to the event, the means by which the attacker committed the crime, and the way the organization responded. To be fair, it is easy to assume the role of the armchair warrior during an attack or the Monday morning quarterback after an event has played out. That is not what we should try to accomplish. Being critical for its own sake helps nobody. Instead, we should take a deeper dive into the particular anatomy of certain cyberattacks to figure out what went wrong and what we might do differently to prevent or at least mitigate the harm that might follow should it happen to your organization.

To that end, I analyzed six major network-security breaches to do just that. It should be noted that I have no specific inside information on any one of these events. The information on each was gathered from what was made publicly available by the victim companies or in news reports. So there is the risk that certain information, not known to any of us as of this writing, might change the analysis.

Dynamic Network Systems—October 2016

Distributed denial-of-service (DDoS) attacks are nothing new to IT security professionals. For several years, attackers have carried out DDoS attacks by directing mass amounts of Internet traffic to targeted servers and taking them down. Companies have been relatively successful in fending off these attacks and limiting downtime. But the massive DDoS attack that was launched against Dynamic Network Services (Dyn) on October 21, 2016, was a game changer. In short, this attack was one of the largest, most efficient, and most potentially devastating DDoS attacks ever recorded. Every organization, including manufacturers, end users, and government regulators, can learn some very valuable lessons from this event.

The Method of Attack

What made this attack different was the means by which it was carried out. The attackers exploited security flaws in common Internet-connected devices that are used in all our homes. Many of these devices, including security cameras and DVRs, come with factory default passwords. The attackers used Mirai malware, most likely spread through spear phishing campaigns, to seek them out, exploit their vulnerabilities, and ultimately control their communications. It is estimated that three hundred thousand to five hundred thousand household products were enslaved to create an army of attacking computers, known as a botnet. The botnet, one of the most powerful ever created, was launched in a three-phase attack over a twelve-hour period. Dyn's servers were brought down three different times during the day.

Why Dyn Was Targeted

Dyn is a domain name service provider that controls the Internet address books of several marquee brands of the Internet. Simply put, in order for users to access the websites of specific companies, the request must first pass through Dyn, which ultimately connects the user to the website. Dyn provides these services to hundreds of companies, including 6 percent of America's Fortune 500 companies.

The attackers knew that by successfully taking down Dyn, they would be taking down scores of major multinational businesses, including a multitude of others that might have been advertising on their websites.

For many of the victims, lost Internet traffic equated to lost revenues. According to a survey Dyn sponsored and published in August, the majority of companies surveyed calculated that an Internet outage costs them a minimum of $1,000 per minute. (Source: http://dyn.com/blog/detecting-and-mitigating-a-cloud-outage-internet-performance-management-in-action/.) In other studies, the average data center downtime is ninety-five minutes, causing an average loss of $740,000. However, if the outage is due to cybercrime or a DDoS attack, the costs increase to $981,000. Moreover, cybercrime represents the fastest-growing cause of data center outages, rising from 2 percent of outages in 2010 to 18 percent in 2013 to 22 percent in 2015. (Source: https://www.ponemon.org/.)

The Expanding Attack Surface

The real concern here is not the fact that a DDoS attack occurred. Instead, we need to realize that the concept of the Internet of Things has become a powerful and ever-expanding attack vector for any malicious actor. The average North American home contains thirteen Internet-connected devices, and that number grows every year. These devices were likely designed with efficiency in mind, as cybersecurity took a back seat. Many are unable to accept security updates. Once a vulnerability becomes known, the owners are at the mercy of malicious actors. To make matters worse, the attackers behind the Dyn attack revealed the Mirai malware code on public hacking forums. This could lead to copycat attacks using the same vulnerable devices in the near future.

The Aggregation of Risk

Amazon, Twitter, Airbnb, Kayak, GitHub, Shopify, the *Wall Street Journal*, the *New York Times*, and PayPal were among hundreds of companies directly affected by the attack on Dyn. In fact, users around the globe were unable to access at least twelve hundred web domains. This made many companies realize that their cybersecurity exposure expanded far beyond their own four walls. Hundreds of companies were relying on the critical services of *one vendor*. If Dyn had not been able to recover from the attack, the cumulative effect could have been disastrous to hundreds of companies and could have affected international economies.

As the details of the Dyn DDoS attack continue to emerge, we can all use this event as a warning and a valuable learning tool. Organizations need to adapt to this and other types of cyberattacks before they occur and as they unfold. Manufacturers will need to implement cybersecurity at the design stage, and end users of IoT devices will need to become better educated and weigh the inherent risks that might come with IoT efficiency. Finally, regulators will need to play some role in clearly defining minimum cybersecurity standards that can be followed to help prevent an attack from happening in the first place.

Target—November 2013

The 2013 holiday season was a terrible one for Target. Not for lack of sales but because of one of the largest and most damaging cyberattacks ever on a retailer. A cyberattack that began on November 27, 2013, led to the exfiltration of 110 million records, including 40 million payment cards. Target took aggressive discounts during what was left of the holiday season in an effort to win back customers, while its stock price was, at least in the short term, negatively affected. Both the CEO and CIO were relieved of their duties in the weeks following the attack.

Costs related to this event have amounted to nearly $300 million and continue to mount. Ultimately, the Target cyber heist was probably the one that first put cyber risk on the radar of retailers and the public at large.

How the Hackers Got In

Security researcher Brian Krebs investigated the Target attack early on and found that a basic information search would have revealed a great deal about Target's relationships with several vendors. According to Krebs, "A simple Google search turns up Target's Supplier Portal, which includes a wealth of information for new and existing vendors and suppliers about how to interact with the company, submit invoices, etc." (Source:http://krebsonsecurity.com/2014/02/email-attack-on-vendor-set-up-breach-at-target/.)

Hackers focused on an HVAC vendor, Fazio Mechanical, and sent a spear phishing e-mail to at least one Fazio Mechanical employee. Once the unsuspecting employee clicked on a malicious link or attachment, Citadel, a variant of the Zeus banking trojan, was installed on Fazio Mechanical computers. This malicious software allowed the attackers to harvest Fazio Mechanical's login credentials and ultimately use these to access Target's networks.

According to an article in *Bloomberg Business*, Target took steps to install a FireEye malware detection tool prior to the attack. The tool set off an alarm when the attack began, but warnings went unheeded. (Source: https://www.bloomberg.com/news/articles/2014-03-13/target-missed-warnings-in-epic-hack-of-credit-card-data.)

The next step for the hackers was to target the point-of-sale (POS) systems. The malware would then perform "RAM-scraping" to steal payment-card information from the memory of POS devices when cards were swiped. Finally, the hackers moved the stolen data to their ownoff-site servers.

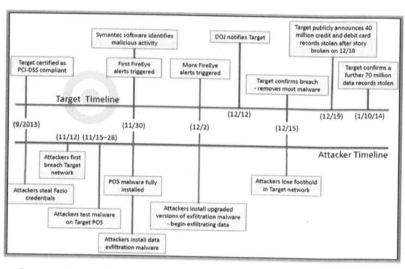

Source: Committee on Commerce, Science, and Transportation, "A 'Kill Chain' Analysis of the 2013 Target Data Breach."

Lessons Learned—Missed Signals and Vendor Management

Target documented the lessons learned from this attack on its corporate web page, which highlights several changes to its security practices. Many organizations can follow these guidelines as well:

- Improve monitoring and logging of system activity.
- Install application whitelisting POS systems.
- Implement POS management tools.
- Improve firewall rules and policies.
- Limit or disable vendor access to networks.
- Disable, reset, or reduce privileges on personnel and contractor accounts.
- Use two-factor authentication and password vaults.
- Train individuals on password rotation.

If other retailers follow the fundamental security practices detailed by Target, it could help address the vulnerabilities exploited during the attack. A particular focus on vendor management should be emphasized. Certain vendors, like HVAC vendors, may seem innocuous to cyber risk on the surface. However, as Target learned the hard way, they may provide a direct route into an organization's networks.

Yahoo—December 2016

As investment bankers and their lawyers pore over the details of a potential corporate merger, a new and troubling issue has emerged that could affect the terms of the deal or even derail it altogether. Cyber risk is now a top agenda item not only for the deal makers but also for shareholders, regulators, and insurance companies. Just ask Verizon, who agreed to acquire Yahoo's core Internet business in a $4.8 billion deal in July of 2016.

Soon after the deal was reached, Yahoo made two unsettling announcements. In September 2016 it revealed that five hundred million Yahoo user accounts were breached by hackers in 2014. Then in December 2016 the company revealed a separate, larger data breach involving one billion user accounts that took place in 2013. After the second announcement, Yahoo's shares fell 6 percent while more than forty lawsuits were filed by customers around the world. Verizon threatened litigation and demanded major concessions on the final price of the deal. Verizon argued that these cyberattacks materially diminished the value of Yahoo.

Ultimately the deal was completed, but Yahoo had to lower its acquisition price by a staggering $350 million. In addition, CEO Marissa Mayer agreed to give up her 2017 equity compensation. The exact equity compensation amount was not announced. However, Mayer's current employment agreement with Yahoo indicates an anticipated $2 million bonus, an annual stock grant worth at least $12 million, and an annual base salary of $1 million. (Source: http://www.smh.com.au/technology/technology-news/yahoo-data-breach-fallout-top-lawyer-resigns-ceo-mayer-loses-bonus-20170302-guoxzl.html.)

Lesson Learned: Cyber Risk as an M&A Agenda Item

While assumption of risk is nothing new to an acquiring company, assuming cyber risk raises a whole new set of concerns that must be addressed early in the M&A process. Specific industries, such as health care, financial services, and retail, might require detailed attention to data risk as it applies to HIPAA standards, financial regulation, and PCI compliance. A thorough analysis of the target company's network systems needs to be part of the due-diligence process and may require the services of a network-assessment vendor. Insufficient cybersecurity and the need for significant remediation of these networks could lead to unforeseen expense and may be a consideration in final negotiations of the target price. Undisclosed data breaches can result in hundreds of millions of dollars in legal costs, regulatory fines, investigation costs, and other expenses. Increased regulatory risk for the acquiring company should also be of concern. Regulators in the United States and around the world have been laser-focused on privacy matters and have made their authority known.

One method of providing protection for the acquiring company would be to enter into a cybersecurity indemnity agreement with the targeted company. The agreement can exist for a period after closing, but there should be an expectation that after a specified time, the agreement will expire. The amount of time should be enough to remediate and integrate the target company's IT networks. The liability protections should be as broad as possible and include all directors and officers, who are often named in derivative lawsuits in the aftermath of a data breach. The agreement should address the many different actions that might be required after a network intrusion of the target company. Costs related to defense attorneys, IT forensic firms, credit-monitoring vendors, call centers, public-relations companies, and settlements should be anticipated. The firms to be hired, the rates they will charge, and the terms of reimbursement to the acquiring company should be outlined in the agreement.

Impacts on Insurance

As discussed in the prior chapter, many businesses have also turned to cyber insurance as a means to transfer cyber risk. Cyber policies typically cover a named insured and any subsidiaries at the time of policy inception. Parties in a merger should be aware that M&A activity will likely have an impact on existing cyber insurance policies and often requires engagement with insurance companies. When an insured makes an acquisition during the policy term, the insurance carrier often requires notification of the transaction pursuant to the terms specifically outlined in its policy. Since cyber insurance policies are written on manuscript forms, there is no one standard notification requirement, and compliance terms will vary from insurance company to insurance company. If the target company has revenues or assets over a certain threshold, the named insured may be required to

- provide written notice to its insurance carrier before closing;
- include detailed information of the newly acquired entity;
- obtain the insurer's written consent for coverage under the policy;
- agree to pay an additional premium; and
- be subject to additional policy terms.

Cyber risk can have a huge impact on any M&A activity. Legal liability and the means to transfer it should be top priorities during the transaction. Existing insurance coverage will likely be affected. All parties need to focus on their rights and responsibilities and engage the right experts to maximize protections in the process.

The NSA and Edward Snowden—May 2013

People tend to fall into one of two camps as they sum up their analysis of Edward Snowden. Many view him as one of the worst traitors the United States has ever produced. A man entrusted with some of our government's most classified information abused his powers. He intentionally exploited closely guarded intelligence that was meant to protect us from external threats. Now that he has exposed them to the world, our government is hamstrung, as its powers have been greatly diluted.

Others view Mr. Snowden in exactly the opposite light. He was a courageous man who took on Big Brother, an abusive beast that has trampled on our Fourth Amendment right to privacy. Through his efforts he proved that the concept of privacy for everyday citizens was dying quickly, if it wasn't dead already. The light Mr. Snowden shined on an abusive government might just bring privacy back to life.

For the purposes of this exercise, it is best to put opinions of Mr. Snowden aside. Instead of debating the hero versus villain role, we really need to focus on what could have been done differently to identify and contain a malicious insider, hell bent on accessing and exfiltrating sensitive data.

Steven Bay was Snowden's boss while the two were employed by NSA contractor Booz Allen Hamilton. "He asked me two or three times on how to get access to what essentially was the PRISM data—we didn't call it that internally, but that's kind of what everyone knows it is. That's one of the interesting things about his story is that people don't realize, he never actually had access to any of that data. All of the quote domestic collection stuff that he revealed, he never had access to that. So he didn't understand the oversight and compliance, he didn't understand the rules for handling it, and he didn't understand the processing of it," Bay said. According to Bay, Snowden "simply grabbed some PowerPoints" and "released those to the world."

In an interview with the *South China Morning Post* on June 12, 2013, Snowden revealed, "My position with Booz

Allen Hamilton granted me access to lists of machines all over the world the NSA hacked…That is why I accepted that position about three months ago."

Bay felt an overwhelming sense of failure and fear of what might happen to him as a result. Upon learning what happened, he said he broke down and cried, feeling like it "was the end of the world." He went on to explain, "Every negative thought a person could have came to me. It was selfish thoughts like—I'm going to lose my family, I'm going to lose my job, I'm going to go to jail, I'm going to be blamed, I'm going to be the fall guy—to thoughts about what does this do to NSA, are people's lives going to be lost, are agents going to be compromised to concerns about my employees, my staff, people who rely on me for jobs. Are we all going to be fired? All these things collapsed in my mind."

Bay revealed some lessons learned from the ordeal that demonstrated how a malicious insider can do far greater damage than an external hacker. There are several things organizations must do to help prevent sensitive-data leakage and manage an insider threat, including

- digitally classifying data and tracking all its movement;
- employing network monitoring systems that send real-time alerts when classified data leaves the network; and
- blocking file-sharing websites that are not specifically preapproved by the organization.

(Source: https://www.thecipherbrief.com/article/exclusive/
first-cipher-brief-snowdens-boss-shares-lessons-
learned-1095.)

Ashley Madison—July 2015

Ashley Madison was a company that was built on the premise of guaranteed privacy. Their client base was married people who, through the Ashley Madison platform, sought to carry out extramarital affairs with other married people with the same goal. Without privacy, their business model would not exist. Ashley Madison was, by all accounts, a successful company with thirty-seven million paid subscribers.

In July 2015, news broke that would change lives and threaten the very existence of the company. Ashley Madison was attacked by a hacking group who claimed they had control of all thirty-seven million Ashley Madison customers. They demanded that the company remove their online presence completely. Failure to comply with the hackers' demands meant one thing: all thirty-seven million members' data would be released to the public. For Ashley Madison's customers, this threat, if carried out, would go way beyond identity theft and harmed credit histories. It would lead to certain divorce, broken homes, and public shame.

If you were Ashley Madison's CEO, with all your clients' personal lives left hanging in the balance, what would you do?

If you complied with the hackers' demand, you effectively put your company out of business. If you didn't, you rolled the dice and hoped the hacker did not carry out the threat.

The CEO decided to stand firm and let the website remain active. He rolled the dice hard. And he lost the bet of his life.

The hackers ultimately revealed all thirty-seven million customers' personal information and financial transactions. It led to the expected divorces and chaos, culminating in at least one suicide. The CEO was relieved of his job and dragged into civil court.

The FTC Settlement

On December 14, 2016, the FTC, in conjunction with the Office of the Privacy Commissioner of Canada, the Office of the Australian Information Commissioner, and a coalition of thirteen state regulators, announced the details of a settlement with Ashley Madison. (Source: https://www.ftc.gov/news-events/press-releases/2016/12/operators-ashleymadisoncom-settle-ftc-state-charges-resulting.)

According to the complaint, the Ashley Madison operators deceived their website users in several ways. These included

- posting fake profiles of attractive women on the website to encourage men to become paid members;

- retaining consumers' personal information after they requested the "full delete" option to remove their profiles, photos, messages, and any other personally identifiable information; and
- advertising the website as secure, risk free, and completely anonymous.

The complaint also alleged that the operators committed unfair trade practices by failing to have in place a written information-security policy, implement reasonable access controls, or monitor the security of the AshleyMadison.com website effectively.

In the settlement with regulators, the various Ashley Madison "operators" agreed to each pay $828,500 to the FTC and the coalition of states. They also agreed to change their practices, to not make any misrepresentations regarding their websites or mobile applications, and to create and implement a written information-security program that will require them to

- designate an employee or employees to coordinate and be responsible for the information-security program;
- identify the internal and external risks to the security, confidentiality, and integrity of personal information they retain;
- develop and implement reasonable safeguards to control the risks identified through risk assessment and perform regular testing or monitoring of the

effectiveness of the safeguards' key controls, systems, and procedures;

- develop a program to select and retain service providers capable of appropriately safeguarding personal information;

- evaluate and adjust the information-security program in light of security testing and monitoring or any material changes to their operations or business arrangements; and

- engage an independent third party to conduct initial and biennial assessments of the program for the twenty-year term of the settlement.

Ultimately, organizations that hold very sensitive information could find themselves in the same predicament that Ashley Madison found itself in. In most other cases, corporate data such as salaries, contracts, and damaging e-mails have been released. During these times, both the original hackers and opportunistic criminals took advantage of the information contained in the data breach to create additional scams and make extortion demands against individuals. If hackers have your data and threaten to expose it, to what lengths would you go to make sure that does not happen? As hackers, hacktivists, and nation-states take hold of the exploitation tactic to affect the reputations of their targets, this type of attack will likely increase. The more sensitive the data, the more leverage the hacker has.

Further, a hack can expose not only your client's sensitive data but also all your business practices that may not jive with what you are promising your customers. Make sure your everyday business activities are consistent with documented privacy policies and written information-security programs. Regulators will take notice of inconsistencies and dole out what they believe is appropriate punishment for misrepresentation.

Stuxnet—2008 to 2010

A major portion of this book is devoted to US companies victimized by overseas hackers and nation-states from the far corners of the world. But one cyberattack in particular that warrants discussion was widely believed to have been perpetrated by the US government. Yes, the US government, in conjunction with Israel, was allegedly the mastermind behind a cyberattack against the Iranian government. The target was Iran's Natanz nuclear-enrichment facilities, and the goal was to disrupt Iran's ability to produce nuclear weapons.

The attack commenced when someone likely physically inserted a malicious USB stick into a computer that was connected to the plant's computer systems. Soon after, a computer worm code named Stuxnet uploaded itself and spread across the network. The worm then sought out the software that controlled centrifuges. Centrifuges were targeted, since they are crucial devices needed to manufacture materials to build nuclear weapons. They spin material at high speeds to separate their components. In Iran's plant, they were used to separate different types of uranium, which is a key nuclear weapon ingredient. Once Stuxnet was able to control the centrifuges, it deliberately altered their speeds sending them into a self-destructive death spiral.

HOW STUXNET WORKED

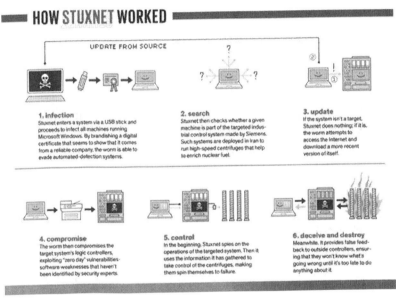

1. Infection
Stuxnet enters a system via a USB stick and proceeds to infect all machines running Microsoft Windows. By brandishing a digital certificate that seems to show that it comes from a reliable company, the worm is able to evade automated-detection systems.

2. search
Stuxnet then checks whether a given machine is part of the targeted industrial control system made by Siemens. Such systems are deployed in Iran to run high-speed centrifuges that help to enrich nuclear fuel.

3. update
If the system isn't a target, Stuxnet does nothing; if it is, the worm attempts to access the Internet and download a more recent version of itself.

4. compromise
The worm then compromises the target system's logic controllers, exploiting "zero day" vulnerabilities-software weaknesses that haven't been identified by security experts.

5. control
In the beginning, Stuxnet spies on the operations of the targeted system. Then it uses the information it has gathered to take control of the centrifuges, making them spin themselves to failure.

6. deceive and destroy
Meanwhile, it provides false feedback to outside controllers, ensuring that they won't know what's going wrong until it's too late to do anything about it.

(Source: http://spectrum.ieee.org/telecom/security/the-real-story-of-stuxnet/Illustration: L-Dopa.)

This was a game changer in that we saw for the first time how cyber weapons can be used to carry out military-style attacks on a foreign country. Cyberattacks historically affected digital assets. This time, a cyber hack affected the physical world. It was no longer a Hollywood movie. It was real. It became *very* real for Iran, whose nuclear program, by some estimates, was set back by as much as two years. We came to realize that if a computer worm could cause so much physical damage to critical infrastructure, couldn't it happen anywhere and be carried out by others? If so, could this type of attack lead to loss of life? This was, by all accounts, a true and frightening turning point for the world's geopolitical conflicts.

Iran's nuclear-enrichment facility at Natanz.
(Credit: Hasan Sarbakhshian/Associated Press)
geopolitical conflicts.

But before we jump too far ahead, a key takeaway from Stuxnet is to understand how the damage might have been mitigated. The genius behind this cyberattack was the ability of the attackers to conceal themselves as the attack was going on. According to the *New York Times*, the initial centrifuge breakdowns were designed to appear to be minor random accidents, with code variations that prompted different breakdowns. During the attacks, the program deliberately sent signals to the Natanz control room indicating that everything was operating normally. The attacks continued from 2008 through 2010. In the summer of 2010, a new version of the worm was developed. As a result, one thousand of the five thousand centrifuges were taken out at the plant. (Source: http://www.nytimes.com/interactive/2012/06/01/world/middleeast/how-a-secret-cyberwar-program-worked.html?_r=0.)

Businesses would be wise to research and consider investing in resources that provide the latest intrusion-detection systems that might alert in real time. According to the SANS Institute, a good intrusion-detection system should

- monitor and analyze both user and system activities;
- analyze system configurations and vulnerabilities;
- assess system and file integrity;
- recognize patterns of typical attacks;
- provide analysis of abnormal activity patterns; and
- track user policy violations.

(Source: https://www.sans.org/reading-room/whitepapers/detection/choosing-intrusion-detection-system-suits-organization-82.)

There are also many free and fee-based intrusion-detection systems available. So start researching those first.

Sony—November 2014

Sony experienced a devastating cyberattack that, according to FBI sources, was perpetrated by the government of North Korea. The *New York Times*'s investigation revealed that the hackers harvested login credentials from systems administrators, which gave them extensive access to Sony's networks. Another investigation by the *Wall Street Journal* revealed that hackers exploited an firewall that was left unattended while Sony moved IT resources from an outside firm to an internal team.

Nation-state attacks are nothing new. But what made this attack different was that it was not motivated by intelligence gathering, intellectual property, or data theft, as countless others were. Instead, North Korea was driven by its outrage at Sony for producing a movie called *The Interview* that poked fun at their ruler, Kim Jong Un. The result was Sony being effectively knocked offline for several weeks. In addition, hackers dumped sensitive information, including salaries, e-mails, medical records, and five unreleased Sony movies online for the world to see. Hackers warned that this was just the beginning. If *The*

Interview was released in theaters, hackers threatened physical attacks on the movie theaters themselves. This prompted the four largest movie theaters in the United States to refuse to show the film. Then, a debate began to rage regarding freedom of speech, with President Obama stating, "We cannot have a dictator imposing censorship in the United States."

Looking back at the Sony cyberattack, we can focus on lessons to be learned on a number of issues, including technical defense failures and First Amendment rights. But one important aspect to take away from this incident is for organizations to understand the consequences of producing a product or performing a service that might offend a particular hacking group. A product or service can get some unwanted attention from foreign nations or local hacktivists. Competing cultures and political agendas will have to be weighed and may not be readily apparent until the product or service is marketed. The risk of hacking is yet one more element of a cost-benefit analysis for an organization to consider before moving forward with a new product, service, or initiative.

CHAPTER 9

The Future of Cyber Risk and the Internet of Things

We have not had a very long history with all the issues related to cyber risk. But the incidents of the past few years have raised great concern, cost companies millions of dollars, and cost CEOs their jobs. Cyber risk has forced us to look inward at our own vulnerabilities and to look outward for help. It has also forced us to look to the future to try and figure out the best way forward in a landscape full of live cyber landmines. Today, there are certainly more questions than answers for the three billion people who use the Internet.

The Internet of Things

Every one of us lives in a brave new world of interconnectivity. For most of us, our first foray into the online world occurred at work, as business discovered the Internet provided a means to efficiencies that made them more competitive. The convenience of the Internet has spilled over into our personal lives in dramatic fashion. The average home contains thirteen Internet-connected devices, and that number is growing fast. It has given birth to the term we know today as the Internet of Things (IoT). According to the FTC's 2015 staff report, *Internet of Things: Privacy and Security in an Interconnected World*, the number of Internet-connected devices surpassed the number of people living on Earth several years ago. As of 2015 there were an estimated twenty-five billion Internet-connected devices. The FTC estimates that this number will double to fifty billion by 2020. (Source: https://www.ftc.gov/system/files/documents/reports/federal-trade-commission-staff-report-november-2013-workshop-entitled-internet-things-privacy/150127iotrpt.pdf.)

Consumers love the convenience that these products bring, and manufacturers recognize this. There has been a tremendous rush to the market, as everything from security cameras, DVRs, routers, TVs, cars, thermostats, and children's toys are being designed to connect to the Internet. The list grows daily. Unfortunately, recent history has shown that, as manufacturers hurry to capture their share of the market for these devices, many have ignored the concept of security at the design stage. Instead, the focus was to get products manufactured quickly and economically. Extra steps in the product design stage, such as addressing security, would likely increase design time, make products more difficult for the consumer to set up, and ultimately increase cost. As a result, many products in our homes lack basic cybersecurity controls and are subject to online threats, as demonstrated earlier in this book by the Dynamic Network Systems attack in October 2016. Many products come with easily guessed passwords or none at all. When security flaws are recognized by manufacturers, they are often not easily patchable.

The FTC has taken notice and made its concerns heard in January 2017 by filing a lawsuit against Taiwanese D-Link Corp and its US subsidiary, D-Link Systems Inc. In the complaint the FTC alleges the company made deceptive claims about the security of its products and engaged in unfair practices that put US consumers' privacy at risk. D-Link sells networking equipment that integrates consumers' home networks, such as routers, Internet protocol (IP) cameras, baby monitors, and home security cameras. These devices allow consumers to do things like monitor their homes and children in real time. Consumers simply access the live feeds from their home cameras using their mobile devices or any computer.

The crux of the lawsuit alleges that D-Link failed to protect its consumers from "widely known and reasonably foreseeable risks of unauthorized access." There are several allegations made by the FTC in which they allege D-Link failed to do the following:

- Take reasonable software testing and remediation measures to protect its routers and IP cameras against well-known and easily preventable software security flaws that would potentially allow remote attackers to gain control of consumers' devices.

- Take reasonable steps to maintain the confidentiality of the "signature" key that D-Link used, which resulted in the exposure of the private key on a public website for approximately six months.
- Use free software, available since at least 2008, to secure users' mobile app login credentials, instead storing those credentials in clear, readable text on users' mobile devices.

(Source: https://www.dataprivacymonitor.com/enforcement/ ftc-goes-after-iot-device-manufacturer-for-alleged-security-vulnerabilities-in-routers-ip-cameras/.)

The case is especially noteworthy since the FTC is not alleging a known breach of security in D-Link devices. Instead, it appears to be taking proactive measures against the company and not waiting for a successful cyberattack to occur before acting. So we can refer back to the FTC 2015 staff report *Internet of Things: Privacy and Security in an Interconnected World* for guidance. In that report, the following recommendations are made by the FTC:

- Build security measures into devices from the outset and at every stage of development—don't wait to implement retroactive security measures after the devices have already been produced and sold.
- Consistently maintain up-to-date software to secure consumer personal information, and ensure

regular software testing. Any identified vulnerabilities should be remediated promptly, connected devices should be monitored throughout their life cycles, and security patches should be issued to cover known risks.

- Take steps to implement reasonable access-control measures for IoT devices, including making sure proprietary device signatures remain confidential.
- Accurately describe the products' safety and security features in marketing and promotional materials.

Big-Data Collection

As we continue to peer further into the future of cyber risk, and new IoT devices fill our homes, it is becoming clearer that threats to privacy will manifest in the form of big-data collection. Big-data collection practices have historically been used by businesses for marketing purposes. It is no coincidence that, after you browse a product online, that same product happens to pop up on a side bar as you visit other seemingly unrelated websites. Target marketing, based on an individual's past browsing experiences, has been happening for years. We shrugged it off as, perhaps, a minor annoyance. We put up with commercials on TV, and we are doing the same thing online.

However, new devices and new applications have raised additional, more ominous questions. We routinely and knowingly give away much more about our private lives than ever before. We willingly pay for convenience. In today's world, payment is made not with money, but with our individual privacy. We give up information about our geolocation to get driving directions from mobile applications. As long as we tell artificial-intelligence products who we are, where we are, what we want, and when we want it, we often get it in exchange. Privacy policies that pop up are never read, but we check the box saying we read them, so we can quickly realize the convenience of our digital assistants.

On Christmas morning 2016, many people found a new friend sitting under their Christmas trees. There she was— Alexa, a wonderfully helpful, fun friend who leaps out of the new Amazon Echo upon request. She will surely change our lives for the better, right? On the surface, the answer is a resounding *yes*. After all, our voice commands to Alexa will give us immediate access to the news, tell us the weather, order us an Uber ride, change the temperature in our homes, play our favorite music, and pull up a recipe. We can go on and on. She listens very well. But therein may lay the problem. Where does all this information about our physical activities and our conversations actually go? Where is it stored, and how well is it protected? How is it actually being used? It is doubtful that many people asked these questions as they fired up the Amazon Echo, shouting commands at their new "friend" Alexa. The device holds approximately sixty seconds of a user's past audio, so that it can react quickly to future commands. According to Amazon, the rest of the previously recorded data is erased. The sixty seconds of data is stored on the device itself, not in the cloud. Does that make it more secure? Perhaps, but data stored locally on traditional devices, such as phones or other mobile devices, has made its way into the hands of hackers and other unauthorized parties. It is not impossible for the same thing to happen with our new friend Alexa. Further, she has seven microphones. It is a fair question to wonder whether or not any of those microphones can be tapped by a hacker in real time, who may compile a lot more than sixty seconds of data over the life of our close personal relationship with our best friend Alexa. In essence, we may need to start worrying about the security of data elements that extend far beyond credit-card and social security numbers. Our entire *behavior profiles* may very well be at risk.

There are more questions. Will the next new product be able to physically recognize us with facial recognition software? Perhaps it will learn our preferences and, once recognizing us, suggest music playlists, raise room temperature to our liking, and pull up a favorite dinner recipe.

The Government's Role

Naturally, during times of uncertainty, we look to our government leaders for guidance. To date, we have seen our government certainly try to help in this regard. Unfortunately, there is broad government jurisdiction over cyber-risk related issues, with approximately fifteen committees in Congress claiming some responsibility. There are arguably too many chefs in the government's cybersecurity kitchen.

In recent years Congress has seen a large number of bills related to network-security and data-protection requirements. While most have not gained any traction, the Cybersecurity Information Sharing Act (CISA) was signed into law by President Obama in December 2015. CISA was designed to create a threat-sharing mechanism between the federal government and the private sector. It is a voluntary program in which businesses can choose to share their threat data with seven federal government agencies via a portal set up by the Department of Homeland Security. The data would be anonymized, and the contributing organizations would be promised full immunity from government and private lawsuits that could otherwise arise from sharing this data. In return, the participating organizations would receive unclassified "cyber threat indicators" and "defensive measures" from the government. The threat information and best practices would aim to bolster the organizations' defenses. In theory, they would learn how other networks have been attacked and how others prevented attacks, detected threats, and mitigated the fallout from attacks. Unfortunately, the program was not openly received by a private sector that is skeptical of sharing any data with the federal government. Privacy groups led the resistance, limiting the program's overall effectiveness so far.

President Obama continued to address the cyber threat by creating the Commission on Enhancing National Cybersecurity in February 2016. It is a twelve-person bipartisan group consisting of academics, cybersecurity experts, and leaders of multinational businesses. In December 2016, the commission released its recommendations on how we might best approach cyber risk. Some of the key recommendations in the report include

- training one hundred thousand cybersecurity specialists by 2020;
- developing internationally recognized cybersecurity controls;
- focusing on holding manufacturers liable for vulnerable IoT devices; and
- appointing a formal "cyber adviser" and "cyber ambassador."

(Source: https://www.whitehouse.gov/sites/default/files/docs/cybersecurity_report.pdf.)

Some of these recommendations may prove difficult to materialize. There is already a shortage of qualified cybersecurity experts. Those who exist often move from the government to the higher paying private sector. Hiring, training, and retaining one hundred thousand qualified cybersecurity experts in the public sector will prove difficult, if not impossible. International cybersecurity standard setting will also be a challenge. We already have vastly different privacy laws from country to country. Further, tensions between some countries will complicate the task even more.

Many of these recommendations have been endorsed by other cybersecurity experts, but it remains to be seen which, if any, the Trump administration will implement.

The Concept of a Cyber War

As cyber threats escalate, we have begun to hear the term *cyber war* used to describe what could happen or might already be happening between countries. In fact, it could be argued that with the Stuxnet attack on Iran, the United States and Israel have fired the first shot. Subsequent shots have been fired, but proving exactly whose hand was on the cyber gun has been a difficult task.

The 2008 explosion of a section of the BTC pipeline was only revealed as a cyberattack in 2014. Hackers reportedly shut down alarms and surveillance cameras before pressurizing oil in the pipeline, which caused an explosion that spilled thirty thousand barrels of crude oil.

In 2012 a virus affected Saudi Arabia's state oil and gas company, destroying thirty thousand computers.

In 2014 the annual report of the German Federal Office for Information Security revealed massive damage in an unnamed steel mill. According to the report, malware allowed hackers to take over the digital controls of a blast furnace and disable its ability to shut down, causing the destruction.

In 2015, the US Office of Personnel Management lost detailed information to hackers, including background checks on senior government officials. This information could very well be used for blackmail.

Also in 2015, Ukraine's power grid was shut down due to a cyberattack carried out via the Black Energy malware.

In 2016, hackers allegedly released confidential information that may have undermined the 2016 US election. Some believe this may have influenced the democratic process and the course of US history.

It is widely believed that many of these attacks were ordered by the leaders of nation-states. They have forced the general public to grapple with the concept of how a formal cyber war would be carried out and what that might mean to the world. It is a topic that needs very careful thought from leaders who have the ability to start a cyber conflict. The Internet is the primary means of carrying out commerce, with data flow being its very lifeblood. If it becomes weaponized, the world's economies will be affected and may come to a screeching halt. An attack on one country could cause collateral damage to Internet-connected nations outside the scope of the primary cyber

battle between two battling countries. Unintended consequences could be far-reaching.

It is eerily reminiscent of debates during the Cold War.
Back then, it was primarily the Soviet Union and the US
nuclear capabilities that were in play. Potential nightmare
scenarios resulting from a nuclear war launched by either
side dominated the national conversation. Today, the
stakes are raised in a different way. Cyberattack capabilities have risen rapidly among many more countries than
just Russia and the United States. One could argue that a
dozen nations have the staff and the technical know-how
to launch a significant attack on another country, while
many more splinter groups with political agendas could do
nearly as much damage as a nation-state. Terrorist groups
have the funding and the motives. They only question is
whether they have the technical know-how. If they do not,
it is almost certain they could buy it on the dark web.

What techniques would be used, what the exact targets
would be, and the timing of an assault are up for debate.
One offensive cyberattack might not necessarily be met by
a counter cyberattack. Economic sanctions or traditional
military might could be a form of response. For those who
opt for digital warfare, it could be expected that distributed denial-of-service attacks would be launched against
companies who carry out critical tasks for many other organizations, creating an efficient way to attack one but take
down many. Social engineering might be used to launch
destructive malware. Ransomware without an option to

pay to decrypt data would be another possible strategy. More discreet methods might involve leaking information about political or military leaders or simply threatening to do so in an attempt to blackmail. It is probable that at least some if not all sixteen critical infrastructure sectors would be targeted. Power grids, financial markets, nuclear reactors, food sources, and industrial manufacturing plants would all be examples of targets in the crosshairs of cyber soldiers.

Our recent history should lead us to a fairly easy conclusion. A new frontier of battlefield is upon us. Digital means to carry out future attacks seems to be the way, at least in part, the world is going to settle geopolitical differences. Our military, our government, and every citizen need to ready themselves for choppy waters as they surf the net. The storm is coming.

Conclusion

The traditional enterprise risk managers have a long
list of worries. Loss of senior leadership, reputational harm, technology-change management,
inaccessible funds, utility failure, travel risk, insurance
failure, product recall, equipment failure, and regulatory risk are constant concerns. These risks have been
around for decades, and that time has allowed experts
to develop sophisticated methods with which to deal
with them. Cyber risk, by contrast, has only risen as a
critical concern in the past ten to fifteen years. The systemic nature of cyber risk can trigger losses in each and
every one of the other enterprise risks listed above. A
successful cyberattack *can* lead to the firing of a CEO.
It *can* cause reputational harm. It *can* force technology
changes. It *can* stop the flow of funds. It *can* take down a
power grid. It *can* rear its head in foreign countries. It *can*
force a manufacturer to recall a revenue-producing product. It *can* cause critical equipment to fail. It *can* result in

insurance failure if the proper insurance policy was not purchased. It *can* lead to regulatory investigations and fines. Never before has the enterprise risk manager been confronted with the very real possibility that this many catastrophic events could be triggered *at the same time by one single event.*

It is only a matter of time before cyber risk, in some form, lands at your doorstep. The time is now to begin the process of managing it. Claiming ignorance or delegating the task completely are simply not the options that they once may have been. Your employees, customers, business partners, shareholders, and regulators and the public at large all expect that you understand your specific cyber risks. They expect that you devote a reasonable amount of resources to manage it.

Be honest in understanding your organization's vulnerabilities. No organization is perfect, and no organization can guarantee they will ever be 100 percent cyber secure. Know what you don't know, and assemble an internal team to take the first steps in managing the risk. Outside experts in the fields of privacy law, IT security, business continuity, insurance, and other disciplines should be considered to work with your internal team. Getting to know the right people outside the organization may take time. Research an expert's credentials thoroughly, because not all are created equal.

Finally, understand that cyber-risk management is an ever-evolving process. There really is no finish line in the race against hackers. Get to know them by understanding their latest tactics and live by the motto *Keep your friends close, but keep your enemies closer.*

About the Author

John Farley has more than twenty-five years of experience in enterprise risk management consulting with a focus on cyber-risk management. He has counseled both publicly traded and private corporations and has served as an adviser to the US Treasury. He is a frequent speaker at cyber-risk seminars across the United States and Canada.

Mr. Farley has performed a variety of cyber-risk consulting services for clients across many industries, including but not limited to health care, retail, financial services, higher education, information technology, and nonprofit organizations. He serves as a resource for both cyber risk crisis management planning and network intrusion response. In this role he applies extensive knowledge in hacking techniques, privacy law, information security, evidence preservation, vendor management, and cyber risk transfer products to help his clients achieve optimal results in cost mitigation and reputational risk management. He has forged key relationships with law enforcement, leading privacy attorneys, expert IT forensics investigators, cyber insurance industry leaders, and federal government authorities to help organizations remain resilient under constant cyberattacks.

Connect with Mr. Farley on LinkedIn:

https://www.linkedin.com/in/farleyjohn

62167484R00116

Made in the USA
Middletown, DE
19 January 2018